THE BABYSITTING BLUES

Chris and the others snuck out onto the stage. The blues band saw them and stopped playing. "Nobody gets off this stage without singin' the blues," the lead guitarist said threateningly.

Nervously, Chris stepped up to the microphone. "Hi. My name is Chris Parker."

The guitarist followed her line with a fast, hard, five-note blues riff.

"This is Brad and Sarah and Daryl," she said, her voice shaking.

The guitarist played another riff, the bass player kicking in with a pulsing bass line.

"We're stuck in the city." Chris grinned, getting into the band's pounding rhythm.

"And bad guys are chasing us!" Sarah sang, right on the beat.

Now, for the first time, Chris sang the lines, "They're getting me tough. They're getting me mean. They're givin' me the blues." She paused. "The Babysitting Blues." She paused again, "I got the Baby, Baby, Babysitting Blues."

point

A Novel By Elizabeth Faucher

Based on The Motion Picture from Touchstone Pictures
Produced by Debra Hill and Lynda Obst
Based on The Motion Picture Written by David Simkins
Directed by Chris Columbus

SCHOLASTIC INC.
New York Toronto London Auckland Sydney

No part of this publication may be reproduced in whole or in part, or stored in a retrieval system, or transmitted in any form or by any means, electronic, mechanical, photocopying, recording, or otherwise, without written permission of the publisher. For information regarding permission, write to Scholastic Inc., 730 Broadway, New York, NY 10003.

ISBN 0-590-41251-5

Published by Scholastic Inc. POINT is a
registered trademark of Scholastic Inc.

12 11 10 9 8 7 6 5 4 3 2   7 8 9/8 0 1 2/9

Printed in the U.S.A.   01

First Scholastic printing, July 1987

Chapter 1

It was going to be a *great* night. In fact, maybe one of the best nights Chris Parker had had in her whole life. In *fact* — she smiled at her reflection in the mirror, fluffing her already twice-washed hair with a styling brush.

Her tape deck was playing so loudly that the perfume bottles on her dresser were shaking, but she turned the volume up even higher, singing along with the old Crystals' song "Then He Kissed Me." Which, with any luck, was an appropriate song for the night ahead.

Chris danced over to her closet, trying to decide which dress to wear. She had already tried on — and rejected — several, but Mike was going to be here any minute and — the blue one. Long and silky, sophisticated and elegant. A *perfect* dress to wear to the best French restaurant in the city.

She took her bathrobe off and slipped the dress on over her head, zipping it up the back, then danced over to the mirror to see how she looked. Pleased by the results, she took Mike's picture down from the corner of the mirror, smiling back at it. He was *seriously* handsome — maybe the most handsome guy she had ever seen. And tonight they were going to drive into Chicago to Le Ciel Bleu to celebrate their anniversary. She danced the picture over to her closet, looking for just the right pair of high heels.

Shoes selected, she danced over to her bed, carefully lying down to wait.

"*This*," she told her picture of Mike, "is going to be the greatest night of my life."

The doorbell rang, and she jumped up. He was here! They had been planning this date for days, and she knew he would be wearing a dinner jacket, maybe carrying some flowers for her, maybe — the doorbell rang again. She snapped off the tape deck, checked her reflection one last time, and ran downstairs to answer it.

Smiling in anticipation, she threw the the door open to see Mike standing there with his hands in his pockets.

"Hi!" she said, then saw that he was wearing an old, ripped sweat shirt and jeans. "Hi," she said again, uncertainly.

He didn't quite look at her. "Hi, Chris."

"I, uh," she touched her hair self-consciously, "I guess I'm overdressed."

"No, no, I — " He shifted his weight, still not looking at her. "It's just — I have to cancel."

She blinked. "But — it's our anniversary."

"Yeah, I know." He looked in the direction of his car: a red Firebird with the license plate "SO COOL." "I'm really sorry, I — see, my little sister got sick and my folks are going out tonight."

Chris tried to smile, wanting to be a good sport. "You have to stay home?"

He nodded. "She's got the flu or something. It's pretty bad. I was gonna call you, but" — he held up a small drugstore bag — "well, I had to get this for her, so — so I thought I'd drop by."

"I could come over there," Chris suggested. "Help out." She grinned. "We could make chicken soup or something."

Mike shook his head. "No, you don't wanna be there. It's contagious. And — and my Mom doesn't want anybody in the house."

"Oh." Chris leaned against the doorjamb, hoping that he couldn't see how disappointed she was. It wasn't *his* fault his little sister was sick. "Tell your sister I hope she feels better."

"Sure." He gave her his most charming smile, the first time he'd really looked at her. "We'll do the French restaurant thing next week."

"Oh, okay." She smiled back, feeling a little better. "When?"

"Not sure," he said. "Friday or Saturday. Anyway, I'd better go — my sister's waiting." He paused. "You're not upset about tonight, are you?"

"No," she said quickly, then smiled. "Well, yeah. But I understand."

He smiled back. A killer smile. "Girls like you come along once in a lifetime."

She moved to kiss him, but he waved her away.

"Contagious," he said.

"Oh." She stepped back, rather deflated. "Right."

"Right," he said, and headed for his car.

She watched him go, managing a brave little wave as the car peeled out of the driveway. Then, she slouched back against her front door, not even caring if she wrinkled her dress. So much for the greatest night of her life.

It was later, and Chris's best friend Brenda Pidgjocki had come over to commiserate. Brenda paced back and forth, her glasses bobbing in indignation as Chris sat on her bed amid the debris of her dately preparations: discarded dresses, the nylons with a run in them, makeup, curlers, blow-dryer.

"Contagious?" Brenda said, for about the fourth time. They were both seniors in high school, although what with the glasses and being slightly overweight, Brenda wasn't enjoying adolescence quite as much.

Chris nodded. "That's what he said."

Brenda shook her head, sitting down on top of Chris's desk. "He's lying."

"Brenda! Mike wouldn't lie on an anniversary," Chris said.

"Anniversary of what," Brenda said, "Pearl Harbor?"

Chris ignored that. "Since we've been going out. Three months and four days — "

"Two hours, and three minutes," Brenda finished, shaking her head. "I don't get why you're making such a big deal about him."

"Because he's the best thing that's ever happened to me."

"He's the *only* thing that's ever happened to you." Brenda picked up one of the college catalogs lying on the desk. "That's why we have to get out of Oak Brook and go away to school."

"You sound like my mother." Chris turned on her makeup-mirror lights and put on fresh lipstick and more eyeliner. She turned toward Brenda, indicating her face. "*This* is what I would have looked like tonight."

Brenda grinned. "Cleopatra?"

"Oh." Chris grinned, too. "I was going for Alexis Carrington."

"Carrington Colby Dexter," Brenda said instantly.

"*Morel* Carrington Colby Dexter," Chris corrected her, and they both laughed.

Downstairs, the telephone rang.

"Probably my stepmother checking up on me," Brenda said grimly. "She's driving me crazy."

"Oh, come on," Chris said, without conviction. "She's not so — "

"One of these days I'm going to spike her Tab with cyanide," Brenda said.

"I thought she was getting nicer."

Brenda shook her head. "Only when Dad's around."

There was a knock on the door, then it opened, and Chris's mother came in.

"Hi, Brenda," she said pleasantly.

Brenda straightened up, very polite. "Hi, Mrs. Parker."

"Chris, Mrs. Anderson is on the phone," her mother said. "She wants to know if you can babysit for her tonight."

Chris groaned. "No, tell her I can't."

"Why not?"

Chris fell back onto the bed. "Because I want to stay home and be depressed."

"Think of it this way," Brenda said. "Sitting for the Andersons will make you even *more* depressed."

"Why don't you go?" Mrs. Parker said. "You could use the money, and it'll take your mind off things. You can work on those college applications."

Chris rolled her eyes. Her mother was a lot more enthusiastic about the applications than she was. "I can't," she said. "What if Mike calls?"

"I'll tell him you're at the Andersons'," Mrs. Parker said, already on her way out of the room.

"I'm too old to babysit," Chris said after her. *Especially* for the Andersons.

The best night of her life was turning into the *worst* one.

Chapter 2

The Anderson kitchen was in chaos. The Anderson kitchen was *usually* in chaos. The pot of macaroni on the stove was boiling over; the television on the counter — tuned to a rerun of the horror movie *Gorgo* — was blaring.

Brad Anderson, who was fourteen, sat on a stool to watch the movie, oblivious to the impending disaster on the stove. There was a loud hiss as the water boiled over onto the burner and he jumped, waving his hands over the bubbling to try and make it stop. It foamed over all the more, and he snatched the pot up, holding it timidly.

Sarah, his sister, came roller-skating almost out of control into the kitchen from their garage. She was wearing a grey plastic winged helmet, a red vinyl cape, and a grey plastic breastplate over her sweat shirt. The

Terror of the Fourth Grade. A plastic sledgehammer was hooked through one beltloop, and she'd slung a *Gremlins* knapsack over one shoulder. Still skating full-speed, she passed the television, changing the channel to a Thor cartoon.

"Hey!" Brad protested, unable to hit her with his hands holding the macaroni pot. "Change it back!"

Sarah ignored him, taking a large sketch pad and a box of paints from her knapsack. Each of them had a large "Please Return To" address label with her name and address on it. Sarah was, as a rule, very possessive.

"Guess what," she said cheerfully.

Brad put the macaroni pot down on the counter. "Mom'll kill you if she catches you wearing skates in the house."

"She has to catch me first." Sarah said, unperturbed. "Anyway, guess what?"

Brad put a spaghetti strainer on the counter, then lifted the pot up to dump the macaroni in. "I don't care, wing-head. Change the television back."

"The strainer should be in the sink," Sarah said just as he started to dump the macaroni in, hot water splashing all over the counter.

"Aw, *man!*" he said, frustrated. He dropped the pot, the macaroni sliding across the counter, and turned to scowl at his sister.

"But that's not the news," she said, skating out of the kitchen to safety. She grinned back at him. "Mom got Chris to babysit for me."

Brad stiffened, almost smiled, then rushed out of the kitchen. Very amused, Sarah skated after him, stopping at the bottom of the stairs to unlace her skates.

Brad tore into his room, over and through a pile of dirty clothes, toward the mirror over his dresser. He stared at his reflection, seeing that he *was* breaking out a little on his chin.

"Oh, *no*," he said, and threw open the top dresser drawer, searching for some acne medication. *Fast.*

Outside, Chris pulled her parents' station wagon into the driveway. Oh, yeah, this was *exactly* what she felt like doing tonight. Very grumpy, she got out of the car, making sure she had *Cosmopolitan* and *Glamour* with her. Her mother, helpfully, had put her college applications into the bag, too. Seeing that she had everything, Chris pushed up the sleeves of the sweat shirt she'd changed into, grabbed her coat, and walked up to the front door, where she rang the bell.

Mrs. Anderson, wearing a black evening gown and putting on her earrings, opened the door. "Hi, Chris," she said. "Sorry for the short notice — thanks a million for this."

"No problem," Chris said halfheartedly. "Glad I could help out."

Mrs. Anderson closed the door once Chris was inside. "Wait right here," she said. "I've got a list for you."

Chris nodded, sitting on a chair in the front hall, wishing that she were somewhere else. *Anywhere* else.

Upstairs in her bedroom, Sarah lay on the floor, painting a picture of her favorite cartoon hero: Thor, God of Thunder. There were already at least twenty or thirty painted pictures of Thor hanging on her walls. Thor, not unlike Sarah herself, always wore a Viking helmet and a cape. He also always carried a great steel hammer as a weapon. Rather like Sarah's plastic one.

Lowering her brush, Sarah examined her tubes of paint, looking for red. For Thor's cape. Among the paint lay a wrinkled tube of Clearasil.

Brad burst into the room. "Did you take my Clearasil again?"

Sarah nodded, holding it up. "I ran out of brown."

Brad snatched it from her, finding the tube empty. "Oh, great." He dropped it. "*Now* what'm I supposed to do?"

Sarah offered him another tube. "Want some orange?"

"I can't use paint!"

She held up her picture. "Hey, what do you think? I figure it's my best one yet."

"You wasted my Clearasil on another picture of *Thor*?"

Sarah looked at the picture happily. "Thor's my hero."

Disgusted, Brad kicked his empty tube of Clearasil under her bed. "Thor's a *jerk*."

"He is not!"

Brad just left the room, Sarah right behind him.

"Take it back!" she said.

Brad turned, making a moron face at her.

"Take back what you said about Thor!" she said, stamping her foot.

Brad made another face, backing down the stairs, not noticing Chris sitting in the front hall.

Sarah, following him, *did* notice. "If you don't take it back, I'll tell Chris about all those love poems you write about her."

Brad stopped, scowling. "You better keep your mouth shut."

"Chris'd *love* to hear how you draw her name in hearts all over the walls at school," Sarah said, smiling sweetly.

Brad sighed, conceding defeat. "Okay, okay, I take it back. Thor's not a jerk."

"Thank you." Sarah smiled down at Chris. "Hi, Chris."

Brad turned, saw that Chris had been

there the entire time, and almost fainted. Sarah, giggling, ran past him and into the family room.

"So." Chris raised an eyebrow at him, the mystery of the hearts all over her school solved. "It's you."

"Me? Who, me?" Brad almost fell down the stairs trying to avoid Sarah's roller skates. "What?"

"Never mind." Chris started to take off her coat, Brad hurrying down the stairs to help her.

"Hey, you look great," he said, fumbling in his attempt to get the coat off. "I mean, really. Your hair, your eyes. . . ."

Chris shook his hand off, removing the coat herself. "What about them?"

"They're so — so, uh — well placed," he said.

She sighed, taking pity on him. "Brad. Relax."

He nodded, then swallowed. "Let me, uh — " He took her coat. "Terrific coat. That's not from Sears, no way. Unh-unh, too cool for that, it's — "

"It was my grandfather's."

"He has great taste," Brad said.

Had. "He's dead."

"I'm sorry," Brad said, hanging onto the coat awkwardly.

Chris took it back, hanging it over a chair.

Mr. and Mrs. Anderson came downstairs;

Mrs. Anderson holding her list, Mr. Anderson holding *their* overcoats.

"Hello, Chris," he said, looking smashing in his dinner jacket. As Mike probably would have.

"Hi, Mr. Anderson," Chris said.

"Come on into the kitchen," Mrs. Anderson said, and they all followed her.

Sarah was sitting on the stool, watching cartoons and stuffing herself with an oversized bowl of Fruit Loops. The soggy macaroni and water were still all over the place, and Mr. and Mrs. Anderson stopped in mutual horror.

"Brad did it," Sarah said, not looking away from the television.

"Brad, clean that up this instant!" Mrs. Anderson said.

Brad, looking sheepish, reached for some paper towels.

Mrs. Anderson watched to make sure he really was going to clean it up, then turned her attention to Chris. "Here's the list," she said, handing it to her. "If you need to reach us, we're at the reception at the Associates Building. The number's by the phone."

Chris nodded, putting the list in her pocket.

"And," Mrs. Anderson frowned at her daughter, "make sure Sarah doesn't wear her skates in the house."

"That's right," Mr. Anderson said. "Sarah, Chris is in charge now, okay?"

Sarah shrugged. "Sure. Can we go to Häagen-Dazs?"

Mrs. Anderson shrugged, too. "Sure. Just don't go after eight o'clock." She looked back at Chris. "Brad's spending the night at a friend's, so you don't have to worry about him."

Undeniably grateful, Chris glanced in his direction. Brad nodded a sad little nod.

"Also," Mrs. Anderson said, "Sarah's just over a virus, and — "

"It's been two weeks!" Sarah said.

Mrs. Anderson ignored her. "Give her aspirin in an hour and once before bed."

Seeing a candy bar on the counter, Brad reached for it.

"Brad, no chocolate," his mother said. "Your acne."

Brad dropped the bar, flushing, *"Mom."*

"Can I stay up till midnight?" Sarah asked.

"Nine," her mother said.

"Eleven," Sarah said.

"Ten," her mother said.

"Ten-thirty," Sarah said.

Mr. Anderson interceeded. "Sold to the Viking. We *really* have to go."

Mrs. Anderson nodded, putting on her coat. "But no later, Sarah. And no TV after ten."

"But *Creeping Terror* is on tonight,"

Sarah said. "And Dad promised I could — "

"All right, all right," Mrs. Anderson said, letting her husband herd her toward the garage. "But after *that*, turn it off."

"You guys behave now," Mr. Anderson said.

"We will," Brad said.

"We should be home by one," Mrs. Anderson said to Chris. "Take good care of my baby."

Chris nodded. "I'll guard her with my life." She stood at the door with Brad and Sarah, waving as the Andersons pulled the car into the driveway. Then the garage door slid back down, leaving the house very quiet.

"Let the babysitting begin!" Sarah said in a formal, Olympic voice.

Chris just looked at her.

Chapter 3

Now that the Andersons had left, it was time to turn into an authority figure.

"Okay," Chris said, making her voice very businesslike. "Let's get this place cleaned up, okay, Brad?"

As he started to answer, there was an urgent coded knock on the back door.

"I'll get it," Brad said. He hurried out to the back hall, opening the door.

"Hi," his best friend, Daryl Coopersmith, said. He wasn't as tall as Brad, but he was much skinnier, with bright red hair. He was famous for both the hair and the extra-large digital watch he always wore. He tried to get inside as Brad practically rhumbaed with him to keep him out. "You spending the night at my place, or what?" Daryl asked, trying to get past him.

"No," Brad said, pushing him back. "Not anymore."

Daryl grinned. "Chris is here, isn't she?"

"No."

"Yeah, she is — I saw her go in the front. And *that's*," he held up a toothbrush, "why *I'm* spending the night *here* tonight."

"Forget it," Brad said.

"You kiss her yet?"

"Don't be crude." Brad pushed him. "Get out of here, okay?"

"Listen to you," Daryl said. "You fall in love, and suddenly you're a classy guy."

Brad glanced back at the kitchen, hoping that Chris hadn't heard. "I have *not* fallen in — "

"What's she wearing?"

Brad gritted his teeth. "Clothes. Now, get out."

"Wait, you have to see this month's *Playboy*," Daryl said, taking a magazine out of his jacket. "There's a girl who looks *just* like her."

Brad shoved him all the way out of the house, slammed the door, then locked it.

In the family room now, Chris tuned the television to MTV, while Sarah snooped through her purse, examining the college applications to Northwestern, University of Michigan, UCLA, and Columbia.

Brad came into the room, still slightly out of breath from his scuffle with Daryl.

"Who was that at the door?" Chris asked.

Brad shrugged, flopping down on the couch. "Stray dog."

"A *what*?"

"Are you going to college?" Sarah asked, holding up the applications.

Brad saw them and panicked. "You're going to *college*? *Away*?"

"No," Chris said, putting the applications back in her purse.

"Whew," Brad said, almost under his breath.

Sarah grinned. "Calm down, son."

The phone on the end table rang, and Chris got up to answer it.

"It's probably Mike," she said.

"*Mike*?" Brad said quietly.

Chris snatched up the phone. "Hello?"

"Will you accept a collect call from Brenda?" an operator asked.

"What?" Chris shook her head. "I mean — sure."

"Chris?" Brenda said, sounding as if she were crying.

Chris cupped a hand over her free ear to hear better, ignoring the fact that Sarah was rummaging through her purse and Brad was at the front windows, gesturing for some boy to go away. "Brenda, where are you? I can't hear you."

"Chris?" Brenda said, still crying.

"What's wrong?" Chris asked, hearing a

lot of background noise. People, motors, someone making announcements.

"I'm in trouble, Chris."

Chris sighed. "You're always in trouble."

"No, I'm *really* in trouble." Brenda cried harder. "I did it."

Chris gasped in spite of herself. "You spiked her Tab with cyanide?"

"No, I ran away from home," Brenda said.

"You what?" Chris reached for the remote control box, turning the volume on the television down so she could hear better. "Where are you?"

"The bus station. Downtown."

"The *bus* station? Brenda, don't go anywhere," Chris said quickly.

"I can't." Brenda sniffled. "I spent all my money on the cab getting here."

Seeing that Sarah was using one of her lipsticks, Chris grabbed it away from her, balancing the phone on her shoulder.

"Chris, I need help," Brenda said.

That was an understatement. "Yeah," Chris nodded, "you do."

"If I take a cab to the Andersons', can you pay for it?"

"That'll be at least fifty dollars!" Chris said. "I don't *have* fifty dollars."

"Well — can you pick me up?"

Chris sighed. "Brenda. I'm *baby*sitting."

"I can't call anyone else," Brenda said,

sounding frantic. "My father doesn't know. He'll *kill* me if he finds out."

"Brenda — "

"I'm *begging* you," Brenda said. "It's really scary here. I've seen three people pass out, a bald Chinese lady, and there's an old guy outside trying to get in here with me! Can you *please* hurry up and get here?"

Chris hesitated. "Look, I have my mother's car. I can't just drive it into the city." She flinched as Brenda made a sound very close to a shriek. "What? What happened?"

"There's a man with a *gun*," Brenda said. "Get me out of here!"

"Okay, okay," Chris said, decision made. "Hang up and sit down. Do not *move*! I'll be there in half an hour."

"Hurry," Brenda said. "I think he's going to kill someone! Maybe me!"

Chris slammed the phone down. "I don't believe this," she said, searching her pockets for her car keys. "I do not." She found them. "Listen, guys. I have to go downtown. Brad, can you watch Sarah?"

"No way," Sarah said. "What if the house explodes?"

Chris sighed. "The house is not going to explode."

"You leave Brad here and it will!"

"Look, I'll just be gone an hour, there and and back," Chris said, "and — "

Sarah shook her head. "My mother's paying you good money to watch me."

Chris put everything back into her purse. "Brad can watch you."

"Why would my mother pay *you* good money to have *Brad* watch me?"

Chris closed her eyes. "Sarah."

"Well, why can't we all go?" Sarah asked.

"Because — "

"That guy Mike," Brad said suddenly. "Do you go steady with him?"

"What?" Chris asked. "I mean, yeah."

"Do you like him a lot?"

"No." Chris shook her head. "Yes."

"Which is it?"

"Yes, I like him," Chris said. "And *no*, Sarah. Your parents'd flip if they found out I took you into the city."

"They'll flip if they find out you left me with him," Sarah pointed out.

"Yeah, but — who would tell them?"

Brad and Sarah looked at each other, then at Chris, smiling innocently. Batting their eyes, even.

Chris sighed. "All right, all right, all right," she said. "Come on."

Chapter 4

Chris got her coat, made sure Brad and Sarah put on jackets, then closed and locked the front door of the house.

"Come on, come on," she said, herding them over to the car. "We have to hurry." She stepped aside to let Sarah get into the seat ahead of her, shaking her head when she saw the roller skates. "You're not going to need those."

"You never know," Sarah said, stuffing them into her knapsack.

Chris started the car. "If anybody asks, we went for ice cream." She glanced over to see if her side mirror was adjusted right, almost screaming when she saw a face grinning at her through the window.

"Road trip?" Daryl asked.

Brad groaned, covering his face with his hands.

"Where you going?" Daryl asked brightly.

"Downtown," Sarah said.

Chris frowned at her.

"Zippy," Daryl said. "Can I come?"

Brad lifted his head. "No. Go home."

Chris swiveled in her seat to look at Brad. "Who is this kid, Brad?"

"Stray dog," Sarah said.

"Daryl Coopersmith." Daryl stuck his hand in through the window to shake Chris's. "You're Chris Parker, right?"

"Daryl, *go home*," Brad said.

Daryl just smiled at Chris. "You must be a great babysitter."

"What do you mean?" Chris looked at Brad and Sarah. "What does he mean?"

"I *mean*," Daryl stretched the word out, "Mr. and Mrs. Anderson must really trust you, letting you take Brad and Sarah into the city," he paused significantly, "*alone*."

Sarah nodded. "Isn't it great?"

"*So* great," Daryl backed away from the car, "that I'm going to get *my* mother — "

"Stop him," Brad said quietly.

" — to talk to *their* mother — "

"Chris, stop him," Brad said.

"And *maybe*," Daryl went on, "you can babysit for *me* — "

"Chris!" Brad said.

"And *maybe*, we could drive to New York," Daryl finished. "Just for kicks." He gave Chris a winning smile. "You think?"

She sighed deeply. "What do you want?"

"For you to open the door."

Chris shook her head. "Unh-unh. No way."

Daryl shrugged, walking away. "Okay, no problem. I'll go see what my mother's doing, and — "

Chris looked at Brad. "What do we do?"

"Run him over," Sarah suggested.

"Open the door," Brad said.

Chris thought about that, sighed, then nodded. "Daryl!"

He was already halfway across the yard. "Sorry, can't talk," he called back. "Gotta run."

"Get in the car," she said.

"All *right*!" He ran back, jumping into the car, looking very pleased with himself. "Hey, Sarah." He winked at her. "Cool threads."

Looking even more pleased, Sarah straightened her helmet.

Chris turned so she could see all of them at the same time. "All right, *look*," she said. "You guys give me any grief over the next sixty minutes and I'll end your lives. End 'em. *Finito*. The Big Finish. Got it?"

They all nodded.

"Good." She faced front, putting the car into gear, pulling out of the driveway. She was *way* too old for this babysitting stuff.

There was a lot of traffic on the expressway, but Chris stayed conservatively in the middle lane. Sarah had coerced her into tell-ing a story, which she did, feeling more surly and cranky by the moment.

"So," Chris said, well into the story, keeping her eyes on the road, "the babysitter goes upstairs and the sound keeps getting louder. 'Scrape . . . scrape . . . scrape.' Then, the babysitter stops at the kids' room. . . ."

Sarah watched her, transfixed; in the backseat, Brad and Daryl scuffled over the *Playboy* Daryl was refusing to put away.

"Slowly, she pushes the door," Chris went on. "It creaks open . . . and the kids are safely in their beds." She stopped, hearing the struggle in the backseat. "What are you guys doing back there?"

Daryl was distracted by this, and Brad managed to grab the magazine, tossing it out the window.

"Nothing," Brad said.

"Unh-hunh." Chris adjusted the rearview mirror so she could watch them more closely.

Daryl punched Brad's arm. "That was my father's, stupid."

Brad punched back. "Shouldn't have brought it, stupid."

"You guys want me to finish this or not?" Chris asked.

"Yeah!" Sarah said.

Brad and Daryl shrugged. Agreeably.

"All right, all right." Chris frowned, trying to remember where she'd left off. "Okay. When the babysitter looks more closely at the kids, she sees that . . . they don't have any faces."

"Oh, *gross*," Sarah said.

"It's just — " Chris thought — "a pile of mushy goo."

"Like Spaghetti-Os?"

Chris nodded. "Spaghetti-Os with meat. The babysitter screams, and turns to run, but there's this big giant hairy guy standing in front of her, and — he raises his right arm, and there's this big metal hook instead of a hand, and he moves the hook to the babysitter's face — 'Scrape! Scrape! Scrape!' "

Brad lunged forward to grab Sarah's face, and Sarah screamed. Chris winced at the sound, feeling guilty for having made the story so gruesome.

"Brad, hold me!" Daryl said in a quavering falsetto. "I'm *so* scared!"

"Tell another, Chris," Sarah said. "Please."

Brad pointed out through the window. "Hey, look!"

They all stopped talking, looking at the Chicago skyline, bright and beautiful in the dusk.

"Wow," Sarah said, sounding awed. "That's where *Thor* lives."

Chris raised her eyebrows. *"Thor?"*

"Well, *all* superheroes live in the city," Sarah said in a "Don't you know anything?" voice. "Spiderman. Daredevil. Captain America. But Thor's the best. He fights the Forces of Darkness." She looked at the skyline, lifting her sledgehammer in a salute. "Forces of Darkness, beware — here we come!"

"*Bus* station, here we come," Chris said.

Chapter 5

It was almost dark now, and they drove in silence for a while. Then Brad leaned forward, resting his arms on top of the front seat.

"Mike what?" he asked.

"Mike what what?" Chris asked, driving.

Daryl leaned forward, too. "Mike what what what? What are we talking about?"

"What's his last name?" Brad asked.

Chris grinned wryly. "Toddwell. You writing a book?"

"Mike Toddwell?" Daryl said. "You *know* him?"

Brad sighed. "They go out."

Daryl leaned over the front seat, Chris pushing him back so she could see the road. "He's got a Firebird, right?"

Chris shrugged. "A lot of people have Firebirds."

"Yeah," Daryl said, "but do a lot of people have the license plate 'SO COOL'?"

Chris smiled. "That's Mike."

"Hunh." Daryl sat back, folding his arms. "He's the guy who beat me up last summer for touching his car. *Which* I didn't do."

"That was *him*?" Brad said.

Daryl nodded. "You know it. He —"

"Oh, come on," Chris said, taking her eyes off the road long enough to frown at him. "Mike wouldn't do that."

"He would, too," Daryl said. "He kicked me so hard *I still* have the bruise." He lifted his shirt, turning around. "Wanna see it?"

"*No,*" Chris and Brad said.

"Yeah!" Sarah said. "Let me see, Daryl, let me see!"

There was a loud bang that sounded suspiciously like a tire blow-out, and the car skidded wildly to the right, with Chris fighting the wheel to keep from crashing into any other cars.

"All right!" Daryl yelled. "Three-sixty!"

"Oh, no," Chris said, more to herself than anyone else, hearing the steel rim bouncing against the road as she tried to keep the car under control.

"It's just a flat," Brad said, very calm. "Pull over."

"This is great!" Sarah said, hanging onto the dashboard, just as excited as Daryl. "I love it!"

"To the right, Chris," Brad said. "Go to the right."

"Right." Tightly gripping the steering wheel, Chris guided the car over to the side of the road, the shredded tire and rim thumping against the pavement, slowly skidding to a stop.

They sat without speaking for a minute; Chris gritting her teeth and staring straight ahead, Sarah and Daryl exchanging "Isn't this *great?*" grins, Brad frowning.

"I guess we'll just have to change it," he said.

"Right." Chris opened the glove compartment, took out a flashlight, then got out of the car, all three kids following her.

She unlocked the tailgate, then lifted up the spare tire compartment, finding it — empty. *Empty.*

"Where is it?" Brad asked.

Chris stared at the compartment, still stunned. "I don't know."

"Maybe it's already on the car?" Daryl said, helpfully.

Chris gritted her teeth harder, trying to digest this situation. "Maybe," she said. She stood there for a minute, hands on her hips, aware that they were all waiting for her to *do* something. She let out her breath. "Okay, okay. We'll just have to flag someone down, and go buy a tire — I've got my checkbook, and — " She stopped. *Did* she have her checkbook? "Oh, no." She ran back to the front of the car, searching the driver's seat for the purse she now remembered leaving in the Anderson's living room. "I forgot my purse — I can't *believe* I forgot my purse! I don't have my checkbook, I don't have any money — I don't even have my license!"

"Gee," Daryl said, watching her continue the frantic search, "did you forget your purse?"

"Yes, you little cretin!" she said, searching under the seat, just in case.

Daryl nudged Brad in the side. "I like this girl, Brad. I *like* her."

Brad ignored him, reaching into his pocket. "I have some money."

"What, fifty cents?" Chris asked impatiently. "You don't have any money — you're a *kid*." Frustrated, she gave the flat tire a good, solid kick. "I can't believe this is happening, I can't believe any of this."

"She's right." Daryl pushed him off balance. "Don't be stupid."

Brad pushed back. "Go walk in traffic, would you?"

There was a bright, blinding light behind them and they all turned, squinting to see as a large, indistinct vehicle rumbled toward them on the shoulder.

"What's he doing?" Chris asked, uneasy.

"He's going to run us over," Daryl said, "isn't it obvious?"

The vehicle came to a slow stop a few feet away from them and idled there, the motor still running. Then, the driver's door flew open and a huge, hulking silhouette — six, or even *seven*, feet tall — lumbered toward them.

With a squeak of fear, Daryl scrambled behind Chris, Brad staying next to her, however uncertainly. Sarah whipped out her address-labeled plastic sledgehammer, stepping in front of all of them.

"Everyone stay behind me," she said, her voice strong and brave. Thor-like.

Chris yanked her back to safety, then lifted her flashlight, shining it at the silhouette's face. It was a man. A *large* man, with a black shaggy beard and deep-set dark eyes. He was wearing some sort of dirty denim uniform and workboots, with a grease-blackened nametag.

"You kids having some trouble?" he growled. Or mumbled — it was hard to tell.

Brad leaned over to Chris. "Was that English?"

The man saw the flat tire. "Got a spare?"

"No," Sarah said, her voice rather small. *Un*-Thor-like.

The man chuckled. Giggled, almost. "You went out on the expressway without a spare?"

Brad looked at Daryl, shaking his head. "We're history, man."

"*Ancient* history," Daryl agreed.

Still chuckling, the man took his right hand out of his pocket, reaching up to scratch his head. The hand passed through Chris's flashlight beam, and they saw that it wasn't a hand at all.

It was a metal hook.

Chapter 6

"Oh, no," Daryl said, panicked. "We're going to die, I *know* we're going to die.

"Just relax, stay calm, don't panic," Chris said, pretty close to panicking herself. She took a deep breath and stepped toward the man. "What do you want?"

"I want to help you," the man said.

Daryl grabbed Chris's arm, trying to pull her back. "Don't listen to him — he wants to scrape our faces off!"

They all stared at the man. The man stared back, then looked down at his hook.

"What?" He smiled, waving it. "You're scared of *this*? Haven't you ever seen a handicapped person before?" He chuckled again. "You must be from the suburbs." He walked back to his vehicle and drove it around and in front of the station wagon.

As it passed, they saw that "Dawson's

Garage" was painted along the side of it. It was a tow truck.

"I suddenly feel like a total idiot," Chris said.

Daryl reached up to put his arm around her shoulders. "Well, if you don't mind my saying so, you *look* — "

Brad gave him a warning look, and Daryl stopped in mid-sentence.

Up in front of the car, the man had climbed out of his tow truck, getting ready to attach the station wagon to various cables and straps.

Chris moved the three kids up against the car, then pointed her finger at them. "Stay here." She walked up to the front of the station wagon where the man was at work under the front bumper.

"I, uh, I'm sorry for freaking out back there," she said. "I guess we overreacted."

He shrugged. "That's okay. I'm used to it."

"Listen, um — " She moved her hand back through her hair. "I appreciate this, but I — we don't have any money. I mean — if you tow us anywhere, I can't pay you."

The man straightened up, considering that.

"We can't even buy a tire, we can't even — my parents are going to kill me." She shuddered. "*Their* parents are going to kill me."

The man looked back at Brad, Sarah, and Daryl standing obediently next to the car. "Why would they want to kill you?"

"I'm supposed to be babysitting," she said. "I'm *not* supposed to be taking little kids into the city, or — or *any* of this."

The man moved his jaw, considering that, too. "Okay," he said finally. "I'll tell you what. I'll tow you into town. To the garage. We'll find you a cheap old tire, something to get you home on, okay?"

Chris hesitated. "Oh, no, that wouldn't be right."

"What *would* be right? Leaving you kids alone on the expressway?"

"No, I guess not." She put her hand out. "My name's Chris. Chris Parker."

The man offered his hook. "Pruitt."

"Okay." Chris turned. "Come on, you guys, let's go. Mr. Pruitt's going to take us to the garage."

Somewhat reluctant, the other three joined them, Chris motioning for everyone to get in the cab of the tow truck.

"Okay, come on," she said, seeing that they all looked pretty nervous. "It was just a story. Nothing's going to happen. You guys behave now."

"Do I have permission to misbehave if he goes for my throat?" Daryl asked.

Chris sighed. "Shut up, Daryl."

"Yeah, but, what did it *feel* like?" he asked.

"What did what feel like?" she asked, not really paying attention.

"When you shook his claw."

Now she looked at him, shaking her head. "You are a very disturbed child."

Daryl shrugged affirmatively, almost proud of it.

When Pruitt got into the cab and started the engine, they drove in silence for a few minutes, the seat very crowded.

"Hey, mister?" Daryl asked.

Pruitt signaled left, changing lanes. "What, Red?"

"How — " Daryl hesitated. "How'd you, you know — lose it?"

Pruitt grinned, his hook clamped around the steering wheel. "Lose what?"

"Well — your hand," Daryl said. "Was it in 'Nam?"

Pruitt chuckled his gravelly chuckle. "'Fraid not. Was changing a tire on a big rig, the jack gave out, back of the truck fell on my hand and," he snapped the fingers of his good hand, "popped that sucker right off."

Daryl stared at his claw. "What did they do with the hand? Bury it?"

"Naw. Wouldn't let 'em do that." Pruitt's smile was playful. "I *kept* it."

Daryl's mouth fell open. "You *kept* it?"

Pruitt motioned toward the dashboard. "Got it in the glove compartment."

Daryl turned to look at the closed compartment, his face paling noticeably. Pruitt chuckled again, focusing on the road, and

Chris and Brad — who had listened in on the conversation — grinned.

The tow truck's radio crackled. "Pruitt!" a voice barked.

Pruitt picked up the microphone. "Yeah?"

"Dawson here," the voice said, distorted by all of the static. "I just went by your place."

Pruitt stopped smiling. "And what'd you see?"

"You won't like it," Dawson said.

"What did you see?!" Pruitt yelled.

"Well — that car was parked in front," Dawson said.

Growling, Pruitt threw down the microphone and stepped on the gas, the truck leaping forward. Chris and the others were thrown back against the seat, too surprised — for the moment — to be alarmed.

Pruitt steered the truck, and presumably the station wagon, across four lanes of traffic, horns blaring all around them. He pressed the gas harder, the truck fishtailing wildly, cars swerving out of their way.

Chris, Brad, and Daryl hung onto one another in terror, cringing as the truck narrowly avoided accidents; Sarah had the window rolled down, laughing and looking out at the havoc they were causing on the highway. Pruitt, in a rage, was oblivious to all of this, careening up a grassy embankment and onto the exit ramp.

"Stop!" Brad shouted, trying to grab his arm. "Mr. Pruitt, please!"

"Don't you guys love it?" Sarah said, hanging out the window. "This is *great!*"

Chris just closed her eyes. This was a *nightmare.*

Chapter 7

The truck sped down narrowing city streets, into a poor neighborhood. The houses, on tiny plots of land, were small and unkempt, with dirty, peeling paint. The lawns, mostly unmowed, had old cars or rusty pickup trucks parked on almost all of them, or so it appeared, as the houses whizzed by at eighty miles an hour.

They squealed around a corner, the truck barely staying on the road, the station wagon swinging out behind them.

"Hey!" Chris protested. "That's my mother's car — watch out!"

Pruitt jammed on the brakes and they were all slammed forward against the dashboard.

"Can we do that again?" Sarah asked brightly.

Pruitt shoved all of them back, reaching for the glove compartment.

"Oh, no." Daryl covered his eyes in horror.

Pruitt ripped open the compartment, which was empty except for some maps — and a large revolver. Chris, Brad, and Sarah stared at it; Daryl still had his eyes covered.

"Is it a hand?" Daryl asked, his voice shaking.

"No," Brad said.

"Whew." Daryl lowered his hand. "Good."

"It's a gun," Brad said.

"Oh, *no*." Daryl covered his eyes again.

Pruitt leaped out of the truck, the gun clenched in his good hand. He ran to a small blue house with dangling shutters, past a crimson Cadillac parked in the driveway. He kicked in the front door of the house and there was a woman's scream from somewhere inside.

Chris and the others stared out through the windshield, watching in some fascination.

"What's going on?" Brad asked.

There were several gunshots, another scream, and the distinct sound of a fist hitting something. Or some*one*. A man — not Pruitt — crashed through the front window and over the porch railing, landing in the grass. He scrambled up, his nose bleeding, and ran toward the Cadillac.

Sarah yanked Chris's arm to get her attention. "What is going on?"

"You, uh, you familiar with the Ten Commandments?" Chris asked.

Sarah shrugged. "Sure. I mean, I guess."

Chris nodded. "That man just broke one."

"I *hate* it when people worship false idols," Daryl said. "I *hate* it!"

Chris just looked at him.

Pruitt appeared in the broken front window, a plump blonde woman hanging onto his arm. She was screaming, pleading with him, as he aimed his revolver at the running man. Just as he fired, she grabbed his arm, and the bullet smashed through the tow truck windows instead.

Chris and the other three screamed as the bullet barely missed them, then Chris got a hold of herself, opening the door and pulling them all out.

"Where do we go?" Brad yelled.

"Out of the way!" Chris yelled back.

Pruitt was aiming his gun once more, but his wife managed to grab his arm again, the bullet shattering the windshield of the station wagon.

"Hey!" Chris yelled at Pruitt, her hands on her hips. "That's my mother's car!"

"Maybe you shouldn't yell at him when he's firing," Daryl said quietly.

"Right," Chris said and turned just in time to see the other man, totally panicked, about to run right into them. Which meant, any second now, a bullet might — she grabbed Brad's arm, Daryl's belt, and Sarah's knapsack strap, pulling them all toward the Cadillac. "Move it! Over there!" She hustled them inside the Cadillac, just ahead of the man. "Go on, hurry up!"

"Hey!" the man yelled. "Get out of my car!"

They all tumbled into the backseat, tangled and out of breath.

"*Lock* the doors," Chris ordered.

Brad and Daryl reached for the locks which, suddenly, snapped down all by themselves. A guy, probably in his early twenties, popped up from underneath the front seat. He was black, wearing an old leather jacket, faded jeans, and Air Jordan sneakers. He gave them a malevolent scowl and they all screamed.

The man outside the car banged on the windows, trying to get in, then fumbled in his pants pocket for his car keys. Out of bullets, Pruitt tossed his gun away and ran outside. Seeing all of this, the guy in the car dropped back down and connected two wires underneath the dashboard. There was a small spark, then the car started.

The man outside had found his keys, but just as he unlocked the driver's door, the guy in the car hit the gas and the car skidded out of the driveway. Chris and the others — for the second time tonight — were thrown back against the car seat.

The car sped through the streets of Pruitt's neighborhood into an even darker, deadlier side of town as Chris and the two boys tried to collect themselves. Sarah, grinning away, had unzipped her knapsack, taking out a candy bar which she very calmly unwrapped.

"Well." Chris tried to straighten her hair. "Thanks, mister. You saved our lives."

"Chris," Brad said, patiently. "He's a car thief. This is a stolen car."

"No way," she said and glanced at the front seat, where the guy gave her a confirming grin in the rearview mirror. She sat back. "Oh, my."

Daryl leaned over to Brad. "This chick is losing it, man."

"I am not!" Chris said.

Sarah held out her chocolate bar. "Anyone want candy?"

Chris slapped Brad's hand away as he reached for some. "Acne, remember? And Sarah, you shouldn't — " She yanked the aspirin bottle out of her pocket. "Aspirin! I'm supposed to give you aspirin!"

They watched her as she clawed at the childproof cap, struggling to open it. "I'm not losing anything," she said. "I'm still in control here! *Got* it?"

There was a brief silence.

"You know," Sarah said, searching inside her knapsack again, speaking in the exact tone of a television announcer, "beef jerky is really the best thing for people on the go. In *fact* — "

The guy driving made a strange sound — possibly a strangled laugh — then jammed on the brakes. "I steal cars," he said. "I don't steal kids. Get out."

No one moved, and he pushed up the electronic locks.

"Go on," he said. "*Get out.*"

Slowly, they got out, Sarah handing him what was left of her candy bar.

"Wait," Chris said uneasily, looking around the dark, deserted street. "I don't even know where we — "

The car pulled away.

Chapter 8

With the exception of the one streetlamp they were underneath, the street was pitch black. Somewhere, in the night, there was a scream; in another direction, a man and a woman were having a terrible crashing argument, followed by a gunshot. In the alley behind them, there was the sound of breaking glass, then the piercing wail of a burglar alarm.

It was very windy.

"Okay, okay," Chris said, as the kids huddled close to her. "Don't worry. Everything's going to be all right."

A car squealed to a stop next to them and they were about to run when they recognized the Cadillac. The front window rolled down.

"I could have left you in a better neighborhood, maybe," the car thief said. "Get in."

Seeing that the others weren't going to move, Chris stepped over to the car, lowering her voice. "Promise me you won't hurt these kids," she said. "I'm serious."

"I promise," he said.

She studied his expression, then nodded. "Okay. I'm Chris Parker."

He nodded, too. "I'm Joe Gipp."

"Any relation to George?" Daryl piped up from behind Brad.

Chris and Joe both rolled their eyes.

"Get in the car, guys, okay?" Chris said.

They got in the car.

Sarah leaned over the front seat, holding a small plastic package. "Want some beef jerky, Joe?"

"Mmm, boy." He pushed it away. "My favorite."

They drove for what seemed like a long time, Chris too uneasy to ask exactly where they were going. They were in a warehouse district now, the streets completely deserted, dark empty buildings all around them. The car pulled to a stop in front of a warehouse that appeared to be as abandoned as all of the others.

Joe took out an electric garage door opener, pointing it at the door of the building.

"Um, where are we going?" Chris asked.

"Crazy," Daryl said, very grim. "Sort of exciting, don't you think?"

Joe Gipp grinned and pushed the door opener's button.

The garage door slid up, revealing a

brightly lit, active, *crowded* work area. Joe drove the Cadillac slowly inside. It was very noisy, with almost a symphony of saws, high-powered drills, and revving engines. There were steel girders and rafters everywhere, supporting not only the roof, but hanging sections of cars — trunks and doors and frames and engines.

Men were working in every part of the huge room, shirtless and perspiring, making strange shadows in the lights of many lanterns and blow-torches. Working on Porsches and Ferraris and BMWs, engine parts lying all over the place. In one part of the room, there was a stack of tires twenty feet high; in other sections, there were head-lights and pistons and fenders, all piled to-gether haphazardly.

Then, at the far end, there were rows of finished refurbished cars, all looking shiny and new, with more men polishing and wash-ing them.

"Okay, call me small town," Daryl said, "but I don't get it."

"Don't you watch television?" Sarah asked. "It's a *chop shop.*"

"Oh," Daryl said, obviously still not get-ting it.

"Don't you know *anything*?" she asked, shaking her head impatiently.

"Thor visits 'chop shops' a lot, does he?" Brad said.

"No." Sarah shook her head again, her helmet slipping to one side. "Crocket and *Tubbs* go to chop shops. LaRue and *Washington* go to chop shops. Even Maddie and *Dave* go to chop shops."

"Oh, come on," Joe Gipp said. "I've *never* seen Maddie and Dave in a chop shop."

Still confused, Daryl looked at Chris, who was slouched down with her eyes closed, rubbing her temples with both hands. "I still don't get it," he said.

She didn't bother opening her eyes. Speaking like an automaton, "Thieves steal cars. They bring them to places like this, they put cheap parts in good cars, file off serial numbers, reassemble things so you can't tell what car anything was in in the *first* place — like, I don't know, a clearing-house."

Brad and Sarah applauded her explanation.

"Oh." Daryl turned to Joe, impressed. "Did you steal *all* of these?"

Joe's shrug was modest. "Pays the rent."

"Isn't it kind of — dangerous?" Brad asked.

"I *like* danger," Joe said.

"You should try *baby*sitting," Chris said, slouching lower.

Joe stopped the car just past a long table crowded with men in cheap, rumpled suits. Most of them were smoking cigars, and they were *all* bent over piles of spread-out papers.

A tall, very pale man sat at the head of the table, his face cold and expressionless, listening to a fat man reading from a list.

"Dallas gets the Ferraris," the fat man said. "One Lamborghini to Phoenix. Cleveland needs four Porsches."

"Forget it," the tall man said, his voice brittle.

"But they got an order — "

"I *said*, forget it. I didn't like the way they were running things." He looked around the table with mean eyes. "*Cleveland* is *dead*."

The other men nodded nervously.

A loud bell rang twice and a hulking supervisor walked out to the middle of the room.

"Quittin' time, boys!" He yelled, and the workers dropped their tools, gathering up their gear.

Joe Gipp opened his door. "Okay, hang on a minute, kids."

"Look, Mr. Gipp," Chris said. "We have to take our car to Dawson's Garage. See, my friend is — "

"Sit tight," Joe said. "Don't be scared." He got out, closing the door behind him.

"All right," Brad said when he was gone. "You guys let me handle this."

"What are *you* going to do?" Chris wanted to know.

"Talk to them," he said, shrugging.

"*I'm* the babysitter," she said. "*I'll* handle this."

Brad looked out at the men, a surly, depraved lot if ever there was one. A group of men that *pirates* would be afraid of. "Um, the thing is," he said, "I have a feeling that they might not be very polite to you." He coughed. "In particular."

Chris followed his gaze, then shuddered. "I think you're probably right."

Outside the car, Joe Gipp walked over to the supervisor, glancing uneasily at the pale man at the table.

The supervisor, Graydon, indicated the Cadillac. "Good job. Got any defects?"

"A few," Joe said. Which was when Chris and the other three stepped out of the car.

Joe groaned, Graydon stared, everyone else in the plant stopped dead.

Smiling his most polite smile, Brad stepped up to Graydon, shaking his hand. "Hi, I'm Brad Anderson."

Graydon just stared, his eyes staying longest on Sarah and her helmet, cape, and sword.

"This is my sister, Sarah," Brad went on. "And my friend Daryl Coopersmith, and this is Chris Parker." He looked around, nodding in approval. "Hey, nice place you've got here. Really."

Graydon was still amazed. "Thanks."

"Yeah, it's really, um —" Brad coughed. "The thing is, we sort of took a wrong turn, and — well, if you don't mind, we'd really like to get out —"

Without warning, Graydon turned and punched Joe Gipp square in the mouth. Joe flipped back over the Cadillac's hood.

Chris gasped, pulling the kids close to her.

With an effort, Joe staggered up and Graydon yanked him over, getting ready to hit him again.

"Gee, Graydon," Joe said, his mouth swollen. "Don't hold it in. Go on — get mad."

"You boosted a Caddy full of *kids*?" Graydon said.

Joe shrugged helplessly. "They got in while I was stealing it. I couldn't let them out — they would've been killed."

"We would've," Sarah assured everyone nearby.

"Anyway, so I screwed up," Joe said. "Big deal. I don't know why you're so upset."

"They know where our operation is!" Graydon said. "They could go to the cops!"

"Oh, no," Chris said quickly as everyone in the whole place glared at them. "No, sir. We wouldn't go to the cops."

"And how'm I supposed to know *that*?" Graydon asked.

Chris and the others looked at each other. Then Brad snapped his fingers.

"We could put it in writing," he said. "Everybody could sign it, we could go to a notary public — "

"Shut up," Graydon said.

The tall pale man slammed his fist on the table, then slowly stood up as total silence fell. "Take the Brady Bunch upstairs," he said, then smiled a nasty smile. "We'll take care of them later."

Chapter 9

It was absolutely silent for a minute, then Graydon clapped his hands.

"You guys clear out!" He ordered the workers. "Go on home!"

Without hesitation, the workers scrambled for the exit.

"Get 'em upstairs," Bleak, the pale man, said, several men at the table jumping up. "*Now*."

Daryl nudged Chris. "If we get out of this alive," he whispered, "I'd ask the Andersons for a buck more an hour."

"We'll get home," Chris said bravely. "This has all been a big mistake."

"What about Brenda?" Sarah asked.

Chris swallowed as a man holding a tire iron motioned for them to climb up the steep metal stairs leading to an office. "Brenda's probably better off than *we* are," she said.

* * *

At the bus station, the clock read eight-twelve. Brenda sat at the far end of a row of plastic chairs with small, battered televisions attached. Next to her, a bag lady wearing a large pair of broken sunglasses was sleeping. Feeling tired herself, Brenda yawned, taking her glasses off to rub her eyes. She yawned some more, then put her glasses back on. Except that they weren't her glasses — they were the bag lady's. And the bag lady was suddenly gone.

Brenda jumped up, frantic, squinting around the bus station, none of the blurry figures resembling the bag lady.

Now she was *really* in trouble. Not only was she stuck in this place where who-knows-what was going to happen to her, but she couldn't see.

The men locked Chris and the others inside the grimy little office, then clomped back downstairs. The room was small and cramped, cluttered with old Styrofoam coffee cups and various stacks of papers.

Daryl, seeing the current issue of *Playboy* on top of a desk, glanced to make sure the others weren't looking, then stuffed it under his shirt.

"Well, that's it." Brad sat down. "We're going to die."

Sarah pointed up at the ceiling. "No, we're not."

The other three looked up. There was a triangular-shaped opening in the sheet-metal ceiling, shards of metal circling the hole like shark's teeth. About five feet above the office roof, they could see the dark steel rafters of the building roof.

"Unh-unh," Chris said. "Absolutely not. It's too dangerous. I mean, look at that," she gestured toward the metal shards. "You might poke your eyes out."

"They might poke our *brains* out," Brad said.

Sarah nodded. "Brad's right."

"Oh, no, Sarah, honey," Chris said, trying to be reassuring. "I'm responsible for you. I'm your babysitter, and — "

"Then start acting like one," Daryl said, "and get us babies out of trouble."

"Okay, okay." Chris took a deep breath, then climbed up onto the desk. From there, she pulled herself up onto the file cabinet, just below the hole.

"Can you do it?" Brad asked.

She nodded, reaching up through the hole to avoid the spikes, and pulled herself out onto the office roof. Winded, she looked around, trying to figure out her next move.

There was a skylight several feet away, high above the chop shop floor, directly above the men at the table. If they walked *very carefully* along the rafters, they could make it to the skylight and pull themselves out.

She looked down again. The rafters were *very* high.

"*Chris,*" Sarah whispered, struggling to pull herself out of the office hole.

Chris unhooked the corner of Sarah's cape from one of the metal shards, helping her the rest of the way out. Brad clambered up next, and Chris gestured toward the skylight. He swallowed, but nodded. Then Daryl came up, holding Sarah's knapsack, and Chris showed him the skylight, too.

"No *way*," he said, barely keeping his voice down.

"You want them to poke your brains out?" Chris asked.

"No, but — " He gulped, looking down. "What if I fall?"

"I won't *let* you," Sarah said, with Super-Hero confidence.

They all smiled at her.

"Okay, Sarah," Daryl said. "Thanks."

Mr. and Mrs. Anderson were having a lovely time. The Associates Building reception was being held on one of the top floors, with a beautiful view of the Chicago skyline. It was an elegant party, the room crowded with men and women in evening clothes, drinking champagne. A man sat at a piano in one corner, playing show tunes as a background to the many cocktail conversations.

Mrs. Anderson, who had been calling home on a telephone a waiter brought her, walked back over to her husband, frowning.

"Multiple murder?" Mr. Anderson asked cheerfully, "or did Sarah just cut off a finger?"

Mrs. Anderson frowned. "I got the answering machine."

He shrugged, handing her her champagne. "They went for ice cream — they're okay. Chris can handle it."

"*Sure*," Mrs. Anderson said. "Sarah's probably hanging from the rafters by now."

In the chop shop, Sarah was hanging from the rafters. So were Brad and Chris and Daryl. They moved carefully, hand over hand toward the skylight, each sliding one foot at a time along the beams.

Chris, leading the others, glanced down for a second and quickly looked back up, dizzy. She gripped the rafter with white knuckles and slid forward another step.

Sarah looked back at Daryl, who was shaking. "Don't look down," she said.

He gave her a weak nod, sliding forward an inch.

They crept along the beams, above the table now, the men oblivious to what was happening above them. Chris, almost at the skylight, stretched out her fingers, clasping them around the window sill. Gently, she pushed the window open. The warehouse roof looked very tempting and very safe.

Down below, Joe Gipp glanced up, saw them, and stared. Then, quickly, he looked away from them, not saying anything.

With the window open now, Chris motioned to Brad, who scrambled out onto the roof. Then, she reached for Sarah, hefting her up and out to him. Daryl was next, shakily climbing onto the sill.

Below them, Bleak searched through his papers, then glared at Graydon. "Where's the magazine?" he demanded.

Graydon looked blank. "You mean, the *Playboy*?"

Daryl was stuck on the windowsill. Chris was trying to lift him up, Brad was trying to pull. The magazine underneath Daryl's shirt was jarred free and started to fall. They all stared in horror, then Chris let go of the rafter with her left hand. Hanging down, she caught the corner of the centerfold with the fingertips of her right hand, her left hand snapping back to grab the rafter. Written across that page were names, numbers, and dates. Not noticing any of this, Chris passed the magazine up to Brad, shoved Daryl out on the roof, then vaulted up after him. They were safe. For now.

Below them, Joe Gipp let out a sigh of relief.

"Where is it?" Bleak asked, still searching for the magazine among his papers.

Graydon looked sheepish. "I, uh, I took it upstairs. There was this article on — "

"*Get it*," Bleak said.

Graydon ran for the office stairs, Joe Gipp hiding a smile.

Outside, Chris and the other three ran for the roof's edge, Brad stuffing the magazine into Sarah's knapsack.

"Where'd you get this, stupid?" he asked Daryl.

Daryl shrugged. "Took it from the office."

"You know how much trouble you're going to get us into?"

Daryl let out an exasperated breath. "Brad, we're facing ten to twenty in prison for stealing a Cadillac."

Chris hurried them all over to a fire escape that led to the street, motioning for them to follow her.

"At least in prison," she said, "I'll never have to babysit again."

"You think they know we're gone yet?" Brad asked, out of breath.

There was the sound of a lot of yelling, followed by an engine starting, then the garage door slamming open.

"Yeah," Chris said. "I think they do."

Chapter 10

Inside the chop shop, Bleak pointed at Joe Gipp.

"*You*," he said. "Drive."

Joe backed up, shaking his head. "Hey, come on, they're *kids*. You going to run them down and kill them?"

Bleak's hand closed around Joe's collar, and he brought his other hand up in a fist. "*Drive*," he said.

Joe swallowed, then nodded, and Bleak released him, turning the mean gaze on Graydon.

"We gotta get that magazine," he said. "The New York notes are in it. We blow this delivery and we're dead."

Graydon nodded, very frightened. "If the cops get that magazine — "

"*You're* dead," Bleak said coldly.

Outside, Chris led the others down a narrow alleyway, running as fast as she could.

"Where we going?" Daryl asked, panting.

"I'll think of *something*," Chris said.

In the car, a black Lincoln Continental, Bleak pointed through the windshield at the alley.

"*Get* them," he said.

Joe Gipp nodded, slipped the car into Reverse instead of Drive, and the car sped backward into the chop shop.

"Sorry," he said.

Bleak was not amused.

Joe put the car into Drive and swerved out into the alleyway.

"Oh, no," Brad said, as the headlights appeared behind them, lighting up the alley, the car engine revving.

"Faster, you guys!" Chris said, pulling Sarah — since she was closest — along. "Faster!"

The speeding car was much closer, and they ran around the corner, finding themselves in another, narrower alley. Somewhere up ahead, there was the sound of loud blues music.

The alley was too narrow for the car and Joe stopped it, Bleak and Graydon jumping out. The kids ran faster, but the alley ended in a ten-foot-high chain link fence. They were trapped.

"Now what?" Daryl asked, as Bleak and Graydon ran toward them.

"Come on!" Chris ran to a half-open,

rotted door, shoving the others inside, then slamming the door behind them. The faded sign on the door read: The Teardrop Lounge. As the door shut, the blues music got even louder.

Outside, Bleak and Graydon skidded up to the door.

"Wait a minute, the front!" Bleak said. "We'll get 'em on the way out — come on!"

The two of them ran back down the alley.

Inside, the kids ran down a dark hallway, with dim, bare lightbulbs hanging from the ceiling. There was a door at the end of the hall, with an old clock above it. It was eight-forty-five.

"This way," Chris said, opening the door, none of them noticing the little grey letters that read: Stage Door.

The Teardrop Lounge was the meanest, toughest blues bar in Chicago. It was a large room, with red vinyl tables and chairs. The lights were dim; the air smoky. There was a bar on one side of the room and a small stage at the front.

The room was packed and the band onstage was cooking, playing a street symphony of pounding electric lead and bass guitars, harmonica, and drums. Bleak, Graydon, and Joe Gipp came in the front door, standing in the back of the room behind the mass of people and tables. Bleak and Graydon scanned the crowd, looking for the kids.

Chris and the others, completely unaware of where they were, snuck out onto the stage into the middle of the musicians. The blues band saw them and stopped playing. Then the customers saw them and stopped talking, drinks halfway to their lips.

Chris stopped, the other three crashing into her, and they looked around the room in horror.

In the back, Bleak squinted at the stage. "What the — " He started, then motioned for Graydon and Joe Gipp to follow him, beginning to make his way around the crowd to the stage.

Chris cleared her throat and walked up to the lead guitarist, a lanky, heavy-lidded man.

"We, uh — " She coughed, self-conscious in the silence. "We didn't mean to interrupt your little concert here. We, uh — if you don't mind, we'll just get off the stage and let ourselves out through the front door. . . ." She pushed the other three. "Come on."

The lead guitarist blocked her path with the neck of his guitar. "Nobody gets off this stage without singin' the blues," he said.

Chris laughed nervously. "What?"

"*N*obody gets off this stage without singing the blues," he said, not sounding friendly.

Chris looked around, seeing silent, expressionless faces. "P-pardon?" she said, with another nervous laugh. "You mean you —" She blinked. "You want me to *sing*?"

The band and the audience were silent.

Chris backed up toward the others, who looked terrified.

"They want me to sing," she said incredulously.

Daryl gulped. "Do whatever they want. Just get us *out* of here."

"But —" Chris tried not to panic. "I can't *sing*." She looked at their frightened faces, everyone *else's* expressionless faces, and realized that she had no choice.

Nervously, she stepped up to the microphone. "Hi," she said, her voice louder than she had expected. "My name is Chris Parker."

The lead guitarist followed her line with a fast, hard, five-note blues riff, and Chris jumped, startled.

"T-this is Brad and Sarah and Daryl," she said, her voice shaky.

The guitarist played another riff, the bass player kicking in with a pulsing bass line.

Getting it now, Chris relaxed a little. "I got a boyfriend named Mike," she said.

The drums joined in, the beat heating up.

"It's our anniversary night," she said, feeling looser. "But he canceled our date. We're stuck in the city." She grinned, getting into this, carried by the band's pounding rhythm. "My Mom's car's all shot up."

"And bad guys are chasing us!" Sarah said, right on the beat.

Now, for the first time, Chris sang the lines. "They're gettin' me tough. They're gettin' me mean. They're givin' me the blues." She paused. "The Babysitting Blues." She paused again. "I got the Baby, Baby, Babysitting Blues."

The crowd began to clap along, with an occasional hoot or whistle of enthusiasm, and the kids started to clap, too, everyone carried along by the beat.

Feeling acceptance from the audience as the band played louder and harder and tougher, Chris let herself go, *really* enjoying herself, singing with more soul than she'd ever thought she had.

"Now, I got this friend named Brenda," she sang, moving along with the music. "She ran away from an unhappy home. I came all the way downtown to get her." She stopped, stuck.

"But the tire, it done blown," Daryl sang hesitantly.

"Yeah!" Brad yelled, both fists in the air.

Regaining her confidence, Chris went on. "So this guy hooked us up, got us all shook up, and now we're gettin' down!"

The audience went wild.

"We got the Baby, Baby, Babysitting Blues!" Chris sang.

"One more time!" the audience yelled.

Chris motioned for the kids to join in, and they all sang. "We got the Baby, Baby, Babysitting Blues!"

As the band came to a musically crashing finish, Chris saw Bleak, Graydon, and Joe Gipp almost at the stage, and gasped.

"Whatsamatter?" the lead guitarist asked.

Chris pointed. "Those are the guys."

He looked. "Who're chasing you?"

She nodded.

Bleak, Graydon, and Joe Gipp stopped, feeling the stares of the band and — suddenly — the audience.

"That won't be a problem. Go on." The lead guitarist grinned, a gold tooth shining in his mouth, and gestured with his guitar for the audience to clear a passageway to the door.

The appreciative crowd parted, Bleak, Graydon, and Joe Gipp purposely caught in the crush and shoved back away from the stage by some very big and protective audience members. The kids jumped off the stage, waving to their adoring fans, passing within inches of Bleak and Graydon — who scowled, and Joe Gipp — who grinned.

Bleak and Graydon scrambled up onto the stage to get around the crowd, and were instantly stopped by the lead guitarist.

"*Nobody* gets off this stage without singing the blues," he said.

Bleak and Graydon made a move to run, and then the whole band was on their feet, surounding them.

Because *nobody* got off that stage without singing the blues.

Chapter 11

Charged up with the excitement of success, Chris and the others ran outside, congratulating each other.

"You were *amazing*," Daryl said to Chris, awed. "Like *total* rhythm."

"I didn't know you were so cool," Sarah said, just as impressed.

Brad gave Chris a big smile. "I did."

"Thanks, guys." Chris grinned. "You were pretty cool yourselves. Come on."

"Where to?" Brad asked.

"Let's just get *away* from *here*," Chris said.

Completely lost, they walked through quiet, dark streets, an El-train rumbling above their heads.

"I got the, got the, got the Buh-Babysittin' Buh-luuuuues," Daryl sang to himself, over and over.

Sarah had put her skates on and was skat-

ing along ahead of them, enjoying the
scenery.

Chris was just walking, looking at the skyline, deep in thought. Brad, walking next to
her, screwed up his courage and spoke.

"Chris?" he asked.

She looked over. "What?"

"Can I tell you something?"

She shrugged. "Sure."

"I didn't really know you before tonight.
I mean —" He flushed. "I knew you were
pretty — you *are* pretty —"

"Thanks," Chris said, not really listening.
"Is that your father's building?"

Brad looked ahead, seeing the Associates
Building among the other skyscrapers in the
distance. "Yeah," he said. "But, anyway —
you're more than that. You're kind of —
smart."

Chris stopped. "You know what? We
should turn ourselves in."

"Sure, whatever," Brad said. "Um, the
thing I can't figure out is what you're doing
with Mike Todwell."

Chris heard *that* and frowned at him.
"What?"

Above them, an El-train was just pulling
into a station.

"I'm serious," Brad said. "The guy's a total
loser. Daryl knows it, I know it —"

"It's none of your business," Chris said
stiffly.

"Chris, it's nothing against you, I just — " Brad took a deep breath. "I just think you should give other guys a chance."

Chris folded her arms, frowning at him. "Like who?"

"Well — " Brad hesitated. "Like — "

"Don't say it, don't say it," Sarah muttered, just ahead of them.

"Like — like *me*," Brad said.

Chris stared at him, then broke up laughing.

Brad flushed, very hurt. "What's so funny?"

"Well — I mean — you're just a child," Chris said.

Brad glared at her. "And you're just a girl in love with a jerk!"

Realizing that she had hurt his feelings, Chris put her hand on his shoulder. "Brad. Look, I — "

He shook her hand off. "Forget it."

"I didn't mean to — "

"Chris, look!" Daryl shouted, pointing at the black Lincoln Continental, which was speeding toward them.

Chris grabbed Sarah's hand. "Quick! The train!"

They ran for the El-train entrance, Sarah out of control on her skates, Chris and Brad each holding one of her hands. They made it inside just before the Lincoln got to them, Bleak and Graydon leaping out.

"Hey!" the train attendant yelled as Sarah skated under her turnstile and the others jumped over theirs, running for the wide stairs leading up to the platform. "Hey, get back here!"

"Help me," Sarah said, trying to get up the stairs on her skates.

The other three carried her up as Bleak and Graydon jumped over the turnstiles.

"*Hey*!" the attendant yelled.

The train was still waiting on the platform, and Chris hurled the others inside, as Bleak and Graydon pounded up the stairs. Just as Chris jumped onto the train, the doors closed, and the train pulled out of the station, leaving Bleak and Graydon banging on the sides in frustration.

Joe Gipp, in no real hurry, ambled up to the top of the stairs.

"What happened?" he asked.

Bleak whirled on him. "I want you to tell me all about those kids. Where you found them, where they came from."

Joe backed away, but was soon cornered. "How'm I supposed to — I don't know anything!"

"You know something," Bleak said. He smiled, seeing Joe's nervous expression. "Yeah, you do, don't you?"

Joe Gipp swallowed. "They need to get to their car."

Bleak nodded, his smile widening. "Then we'll get to it first."

The train car was empty and Chris sat on one side, the other three sitting across from her, Brad still sulking slightly.

"What do those guys want, anyway?" Chris asked, trying to catch her breath.

Daryl snickered. "Maybe they want to give us a ride home."

"Right," Chris said.

"You don't think so?"

Chris shook her head, looking away.

Sarah took off her skates, changing into the sneakers that were in her knapsack. The *Playboy* magazine was falling out, and she tucked it back in without looking at it.

"Sarah, lie down there and go to sleep," Chris said.

Sarah looked at her dubiously. "I'm not tired."

"Pretend you are."

"Then can I pretend to sleep?"

Chris rubbed her face, tired herself. "Sure. Whatever." She sighed. "What a night."

The door at the back of the car slammed open and a gang, the Street Kings, swaggered in. There were fifteen of them, wearing black leather jackets and black jeans, chains hanging from various parts of their clothing. They stood there, staring at the other end of the car.

"Oh, boy," Daryl said in a very small voice.

There was another slam, the door at the other end of the car flying open. Another gang, the Black Lords, came in, wearing red leather jackets, jeans, and boots. The two gangs stared at each other, murder in their eyes.

"Could be, they're trying out for *West Side Story* tomorrow," Brad said, with faint optimism.

"Could be, we're *dead*," Daryl said.

Chapter 12

The subway car was absolutely silent.

"Cool threads," Sarah remarked, indicating both gangs in general.

No response.

"How 'bout those Cubs," Daryl said.

Chris shot them both a fierce look. "We'll get off at the next stop."

"Don't you even *think* of gettin' off," the leader of the Street Kings said.

Chris flinched, but saw that he was talking to the Black Lords leader.

"The only people gettin' off this train are doin' it in *body bags*," the Black Lords leader said.

Chris moved over to sit with the others, the two gangs ignoring them.

"Don't panic," she whispered.

"Can't think why we would," Daryl said, perspiring almost as heavily as Brad was.

"You're on our train," the Street Kings leader said.

"You're rolling into our turf," the Black Lords leader said.

Chris and the kids looked from one gang to the other, like watching a tennis match.

The Black Lords leader punched his forefinger into the transit map on the wall. "As soon as we cross Deveraux Street, you're dead."

Chris glanced at the map, seeing that Devereaux was the next stop, St. Joseph's Hospital the one after it.

The Black Lords leader was looking out the window, watching the streets pass by. "Here's Lathrop. Here's Jackson." He smiled a scary smile. "And here we are." The train stopped.

The members of both gangs whipped out their switchblades, murderously approaching each other.

"They're going to kill each other," Daryl said, panicked.

"And kill *us* doing it." Brad said, more panicked.

"Oh, help," Chris said.

Sarah tried to push them out of the way. "Get back — I want to see this."

The two gangs were almost upon each other and Chris got up, stepping between them.

"Excuse me," she said.

Thirty cold pairs of eyes focused on her, knives ready.

"I couldn't help but notice that you two groups of . . . people are about to start killing each other." She managed a flimsy smile. "I was wondering if you could just sort of wait on that until we can get off this train?"

The Black Lords leader held his switchblade out toward her. "Sit down, dog."

The doors closed, and the train pulled out of the station.

Chris blinked. "What?"

"I *said*," he came closer, "sit down, you ugly dog."

Daryl pushed Brad's arm. "You gonna let them get away with that?"

Brad frowned at him, but jumped up.

"Hey!" Daryl made a grab to pull him back, but missed. "I was kidding."

Brad walked over next to Chris, shaking slightly. "You can't call her that," he said to the Black Lords leader. "It's really rude. Apologize."

"It's okay," Chris said through her teeth. "Stay out of this."

"He called you an ugly dog," Brad said, clenching his fists.

"Brad, shut up!" Chris said, her voice close to hysteria.

The Black Lords leader waved his knife ominously. "Listen to the dog, Brad."

Brad scowled at him. "Watch your mouth, you — you big turkey."

It was very quiet.

Chris stood still, frozen; Brad swallowed. Daryl buried his head in his hands; Sarah watched the whole situation with great interest.

Ever so slowly, the Black Lords leader swaggered over in front of Brad. "You just can't keep your feet out of your mouth, boy," he said, with a vicious smile. "Let me help you out." He threw the knife straight down in the floor, then smiled again. "How's *that*?"

Brad looked down, seeing the knife stuck through the tip of his sneaker and lodged in the subway floor, his face paling.

"Don't mess with the Black Lords," the leader said.

Thinking fast, Chris grabbed the knife, hurling it into the wall.

"Don't mess with the *babysitter*," she said, her voice even colder than the gang leader's had been.

All of the gang members stared at her, stunned into silence.

The train stopped, the doors shot open, and Chris drew the kids behind her, Brad limping. Slowly, with great dignity, she backed them out of the train, the doors shutting behind them. The train pulled out of the station, the gang members still staring out of the windows.

"I can't believe it, I really can't — " Chris started, bravado gone. She bent down next to Brad. "Are you okay?"

"I don't know," Brad said, completely panicked, holding his leg. "I can't feel anything."

"Tetanus!" Daryl said. "Lockjaw. Rabies. Scabies. Oh, man, you could get it *all*."

Sarah pointed to the subway station sign: St. Joseph's Hospital. "Should we go there?"

"Yes!" Chris said, and, picking Brad up, ran for the exit. She tore down the street, not even noticing how heavy he was, Daryl and Sarah struggling to keep up. They ran past a row of parked ambulances and into the emergency ward.

The Emergency Room was packed, with patients suffering from all sorts of injuries. Doctors and nurses, working on very little sleep, stumbled back and forth, while patients were moved in and out of treatment rooms.

Chris skidded through the electric-eye doors, Brad still in her arms, Daryl and Sarah right behind her.

"Medic!" She yelled.

Everyone turned, including a man with a broken nose and two black eyes standing inside an elevator with two police officers.

It was the man from Pruitt's house, the man whose Cadillac Joe Gipp had stolen. With them in it.

"Hey!" He pointed. "That's them! They stole my car!"

The police officers looked bored, pulled him back inside the elevator, and the doors slid shut.

Chris and the others neither saw nor heard him. They were surrounded by a battery of nurses who bundled Brad onto a gurney and took him away.

"Please wait here," one of them told Chris.

She nodded, slumping down into a chair, Daryl and Sarah sitting next to her. Exhausted, she looked up at the clock seeing that it was ten-thirty-nine.

"Brenda, if you're dead," she said quietly, "I wish I was with you."

Chapter 13

Brenda was far from dead. She sat in the bus station, holding the bag lady's sunglasses, so blind without her glasses that she couldn't do much of *anything*.

She saw a small animal moving in a nearby corner and smiled. A kitten. It was probably a kitten.

"Here, kitty, kitty," she said, standing up, making her blurry way over there. "Come here, kitty." She put her hand down. "What's the matter, you get lost? You run away from home?"

The little animal sniffed at her fingers.

"Oooh, cold nose," Brenda said. "Now, don't bite. You can nibble, just don't bite." She scooped the animal up, holding it up under her chin. "You poor thing, you're shivering."

"Hey!" a man yelled. "Drop it!"

Brenda turned, squinted to see two blurry

janitors, one holding a box of some kind, the other a broom.

"Put that animal *down*," the same man said.

Afraid, Brenda lowered the animal to the ground. The janitor came at it with his broom and Brenda screamed, trying to stop him, the other janitor holding her back.

"You monsters!" she said. "How could you do that to a kitten? A poor little kitten!"

The janitors stared at her, then laughed.

"What's so funny," she asked.

"Kitten?" one of the janitors said. "That ain't no kitten, kid. It's a jumbo-size sewer rat." He held it up by the tail, then dropped it in the box he was carrying.

Brenda screamed, running away, praying that she would find someplace safe to hide and wait for Chris to show up.

Daryl and Sarah sat on a worn vinyl couch in the waiting room. Chris had gone off to find a doctor and see what was taking so long.

"This is all my fault," Daryl said, shaking his head. "I can't keep my mouth shut. Why do I always have to open my big mouth? I could have gotten him *killed*. What if they have to amputate? Why can't I just shut up, I wish I could just shut up."

"Shut up, Daryl," Sarah said.

Daryl shut up.

"It's not your fault," she said. "He would've done it even if you weren't there."

A tired-looking doctor with a three-day growth of beard and dark circles under his eyes came out of a treatment room.

"Here he is," the doctor said. "A-okay."

Brad limped out behind him. "Hi," he said sheepishly.

"You're okay?" Daryl asked, worried.

Brad nodded sheepishly and Daryl ran over to embrace him. Brad looked at Sarah for an explanation, but she just shrugged.

"Uh, Daryl," he said, trying to pull free. "I can't breathe."

A nurse hurried down the hall. "Doctor, the guy with the stab wounds just died."

The doctor looked unhappy. "Oh, dear, all right. Don't you children go anywhere, I'll be right back."

The doctor and nurse headed off, leaving Daryl still hugging Brad.

"You're really okay?" he asked.

"It just nicked me." Brad's grin was embarrassed. "I got *one* stitch."

"D-do you — " Daryl swallowed. "Do you forgive me?"

Brad looked confused. "Forgive you for what?"

"Oh, thank you." Daryl hugged him harder. "Thank you."

Brad looked at Sarah. "What's with him?"

Sarah shrugged, taking out a piece of beef jerky.

Down the hall, Chris saw the doctor heading in her direction and stopped him.

"Doctor?" she asked. "I can't find my friend."

"Your friend?" The doctor shook his head. "I'm sorry, which one was he?"

"Uh —" She hesitated. "Stab wound."

"Oh, dear," the doctor said.

"What?"

He put his hand on her shoulder. "I'm sorry. Your friend is dead."

She stared at him, blinked, then fell over in a dead faint.

"Hey, Chris!" Sarah said, seeing her from the other end of the hall. "Look, something's wrong with Chris!"

They ran down the hall to where the doctor and nurse were trying to revive her.

"What happened?" Brad asked. "Is she all right?"

The doctor looked at him, and sighed. "Oh, dear. *You're* her friend." He looked down. "She's fainted."

The nurse cracked some ammonia under her nose and Chris stirred, slowly waking up. The first thing she saw was Brad, and she screamed.

"There, there, everything's all right," the doctor said. "I made a mistake. See, he's fine."

"Oh." Chris groaned, putting a weak hand to her forehead. "I had the worst nightmare. We were stuck in the city, and" — she saw Brad's tattered sneaker — "this is really happening."

Daryl grinned at her. "Some night, hunh?"

"You children stay right here," the doctor said. "I'll send the nurse back with the paperwork."

Brad watched them go. "Are they going to want our names?"

"Yeah." Chris sighed. "We're finished." She sighed again. "I'll go call my mother."

"Oh, no, no parents," Daryl said. "We'll be *killed*."

The man whose Cadillac they had stolen suddenly appeared at the end of the hall. "Hey!" He charged down the hall after them. "Where's my car?!"

Chris and the others stared at him, too surprised to move.

Chapter 14

The man thundered down the hall, heading straight for them. "Where's my car, you little — "

Mr. Pruitt burst out of one of the treatment rooms, slamming into the man with all the force of a Lawrence Taylor. Blindsided, the man crashed into the wall, then fell heavily to the floor, unconscious.

Pruitt had handcuffs dangling from his left hand, his hook swinging free, and his face was badly bruised.

"Hey, you!" One of the police officers who had been with the other man shouted, running down the hall. "Hold it right there!"

Pruitt turned to Chris and the others. "You want your car? Come on, it's fixed!"

"Fixed?" Chris asked.

"*Fixed*," Brad said, grabbing her arm and pulling her down the hall after Pruitt.

Both police officers were chasing them now, along with three doctors and another police officer who came running out of Pruitt's treatment room.

"What are you doing here?" Chris asked, as they ran outside, crouching down behind some ambulances to stay out of sight.

"My wife called the cops." Pruitt shrugged. "I just got a little banged up."

Chris nodded sympathetically.

"Where's the car?" Daryl asked.

"I got it to Dawson's Garage. Go past the university to Lower Wacker Drive." Pruitt pointed vaguely. "You can't miss it. I paid for your window — that was my fault. But Dawson's gonna hit you for the tire."

"How much?" Chris asked, dreading the answer.

"Fifty bucks."

"*Fifty?*" she said.

"Sorry." Pruitt saw the police officers running out of the hospital and got up, ready to make a break for it.

"Wait," Chris said. "Where are you going?"

He shrugged. "I'm a fugutive now."

Daryl peeked around the ambulance, seeing the man whose Cadillac they had stolen running out, too. "Kind of like us."

Pruitt smiled at him. "Kind of like you, Red."

Daryl reached up, shaking his hook without any hesitation, and they exchanged smiles.

"Good luck, babysitter," he said to Chris. She nodded. "You, too, Mr. Pruitt."

Pruitt nodded back and ran off, the police officers in hot pursuit.

"Where are we going to get fifty dollars?" Brad asked.

"I don't know," Chris said. "Maybe we could sell Daryl." She winked at him, giving him a fake half-nelson. "Don't worry, we'll think of something. Let's go find the university."

It was a long walk, but after asking directions several times, they finally found it and walked through the campus, looking for Lower Wacker Drive.

"Chris, I need a bathroom," Sarah said uneasily.

Chris nodded. "Okay, we'll find one soon. I promise."

They walked down the dark campus street, fraternity houses on each side.

"Hey, listen," Daryl said. "Rock and roll!"

"Yeah," Brad said, sounding exhausted, "so?"

They walked a little further, the music getting louder.

Daryl grinned. "All *right*. A party!"

They were in front of a fraternity house, Delta Lambda Chi. It was an old two-story house, the doors and windows wide open, students laughing and dancing inside, other students spilling out of the house into the front yard.

"See ya," Daryl said, and headed for the house.

"Daryl, get back here!" Chris called after him, but he had already disappeared into the crush of people. She sighed. "Why do I have this strange feeling we'll never see him again?"

Brad rubbed his hand across his face, yawning. "At least Sarah can use a bathroom in there."

"I *really* have to, Chris," Sarah said.

"All right," Chris said. "Come on."

The closer they got to the house, the louder the music was. Southside Johnny and the Asbury Jukes, a seven-piece rock band, were playing *live*. Chris pushed past the crowd at the front door, steering Sarah inside.

There was a group of guys standing by the fireplace, one of whom stared as they came in.

"I don't believe it," he said, his mouth open.

The other guys followed his gaze, seeing Brad, tired and limping; Sarah in her helmet and knapsack; Chris looking beautifully exhausted.

"So, wait," one of the other guys said, looking at Brad and Sarah. "Are they like, you know, smart? I mean, like — like accelerated?"

"Like, like big I.Q.s," another guy said.

"No, stupid," the first guy said and pointed at Chris. "*That's* Miss February."

Dan Lynch, tall and handsome, probably the only guy in the place who wasn't a jerk, overheard them and glanced over.

"No way," one of the guys was saying. "Like — no way."

"Miss who?" another guy asked.

"Miss February," the first guy said. "It's *her*. Wait, I'll show you." He ran for the stairs, the other guys staring at Chris.

Dan Lynch watched *them*, in obvious concern.

As ever, not really aware of what was going on around them, Chris, Brad, and Sarah stood at the doorway, looking at the party.

"Wow," Sarah said, seeing the dance floor. She sat down and put on her roller skates.

Chris gazed around the room, seeing laughing, happy students everywhere she looked. "If this is what college is like, I can live with it," she said.

"Oh, great." Brad tugged at her sleeve. "*Look*."

Daryl was strutting his way up to the refreshment table, joining a group of jocks.

"Hiya, fellas," Daryl said, clapping one of them on the back.

The jocks stopped drinking to stare at him.

"I must be hallucinating," one of the biggest jocks said. "Is this — a *football*?"

The jocks guffawed, Daryl joining in heartily.

"Go for the field goal!" the same jock yelled, grabbing Daryl by the back of his coat and jeans, hauling him over the table and launching him across the room.

The other jocks laughed raucously as Daryl landed by the stairs, finding himself looking up into the beautiful blue eyes of a blonde co-ed.

"Hi," he said, giving her a big smile.

The girl smiled back.

Chris started across the room. "I'll get Daryl. You take Sarah to the bathroom."

Brad grabbed Sarah's hand, pulling her along on her skates.

"Don't!" Sarah tried to pull free. "I want to dance!"

"We have two hours to get home," Chris said. "We don't have *time* to dance."

"Come on, Sarah, okay?" Brad said, dragging her away from the dance floor. "Try *not* to act your age."

Before Chris could get upstairs, the group of guys surrounded her. The one who had gone upstairs was holding his issue of *Playboy*.

"Look," he said, reading Miss February's stats. "It says here, you love old Tony Orlando and Dawn records." He moved closer, grinning at her. "Me, too."

Chris tried to push past him. "I'm sorry, I don't know what you're talking about."

"Look!" Another guy blocked her way. "We have the same pet peeves. This is *amazing*."

The first guy shoved the magazine and a pen into her hand. "Would you autograph this? Please?"

"What?" She looked at the picture, saw the resemblance, and gasped. "No, that's not — I —"

"Then after that," the guy said, "maybe you and I can go somewhere together. Alone."

Chris stared at him, stared at the picture, then realized that she was completely surrounded by football players. Loud, crude football players. She was in trouble.

Chapter 15

Halfway across the room, Brad saw all of this and tried to get through the crowd to help her, but Dan Lynch got there first.

"Problem?" he asked with a calm, pleasant smile, "guys?"

"It's not me," Chris said, still shocked. "They think it's me."

Dan looked at the picture, did a double-take, and looked at it again.

"It's her," one of the guys said.

"What's your name?" Dan asked her, his eyes — nice green eyes — crinkling with amusement.

Chris glanced down at the model's stats and blanched. "It's *not* Shaylene."

Dan laughed. "No, I'm sure it isn't. Come on, let's go over here."

"I *told* you it wasn't her," one of them said.

Grumbling among themselves, the guys moved off.

"Uh, thanks," Chris said, still reeling from all of that.

Dan grinned at her.

"So," Brad said, tapping his foot, not liking the looks the two of them were exchanging. "Where's the stupid bathroom?"

"That way," Dan said, pointing straight ahead.

"Mmmm." Brad turned, hauling Sarah away.

Dan gestured after them with his hand. "You usually bring your brothers and sisters to these kinds of things?"

"Usually I don't *go* to these kinds of things," Chris said without thinking.

Dan smiled, leaning back against the wall with his hands in his pockets. "I haven't seen you here on campus before. Are you a freshman?"

Chris blushed and shook her head.

"Sophomore?"

She shook her head.

"Hmmm." He studied her. "You *can't* be a junior."

"I'm a senior." She smiled shyly. "In high school."

Dan looked genuinely shocked. "Get out of town."

Chris's grin was wry. "I'm *trying* to."

"I can't believe it," he said.

"What?"

"That the prettiest girl at the University of Chicago is in high school," he said.

Chris grinned. "That was good."

He grinned back. "My name's Dan Lynch. Would you like to dance?"

"I —" Chris almost agreed, then shook her head. "I can't. I don't have time."

"She'll be in line for the bathroom for a few minutes," he said. "There's time."

That made sense and she nodded, completely charmed by him. "Okay. For a minute."

Dan led her out to the floor as Southside Johnny and the Asbury Jukes struck up another song.

"So," Dan said, his eyebrows coming together. "You're babysitting these kids?"

"No one could conceivably call what I've been doing tonight 'babysitting,'" Chris said, dancing.

Dan laughed. "Oh, come on."

"If these kids grow up to be criminals, it's because of me," she said, filling him in on the evening's disasters.

"Everything'll be all right," Dan said. "It's all going to work out fine. *I* think you're doing a great job."

"You do?" Chris asked, not agreeing with him, but happy to hear it.

"Sure," he said, very confident. "You got

the kids *this* far. They're still alive. It could be a lot worse."

It *definitely* could be a lot worse. "You're right," she said.

"Is there anything I can do to help?" he asked. "What do you need?"

"Well —" Chris wasn't sure if she should ask, but decided that it couldn't hurt. "Actually, now that you asked me . . . fifty dollars."

Dan reached into his back pocket and pulled out a wallet. "All I have's a twenty. Wait here, and I'll get the rest." He handed her the bill.

She took it hesitantly. "This is a loan," she said.

He smiled. "Of course."

Chris watched him go, then turned to see Brad and Sarah right next to her. Brad's expression was both hurt and angry.

"He's getting us fifty dollars," Chris said.

"Terrific," Brad said, stiffly. "Swell."

Over on the stairs, Daryl was sitting with the beautiful blonde, who was pouring out her heart to him.

"It's always the same," she said. "*Always.*" She nodded toward one of the biggest jocks, a twenty-one-year-old giant, who was holding a football and surrounded by a crowd of enthralled admirers.

"All he cares about," the blonde said, "are the Bears, the Bengals, the *Dolphins*. What about the love? The *romance*?"

"*I* care about those things," Daryl said, making his voice lower than usual. "Deeply."

The blonde sighed, maybe close to tears. "I'm just so lonely."

"How could a righteous babe like you be lonely?" Daryl asked, shaking his head as though dismayed.

"That's the sweetest thing anyone's ever said to me," the girl said. "I *like* you." She leaned down and kissed him, Daryl's eyes practically popping out of his head.

Her jock boyfriend saw this and thundered over, yanking them apart. "You're dead, kid," he said.

"You've been replaced," the blonde said to her boyfriend. "You big dumb bohunk!"

Ignoring her, he made a swipe at Daryl, who leaped out of the way.

"I think I have to go home now!" he said. He located Chris and ran over to her.

"Where've *you* been?" she asked.

"Out of my league," he said, glancing over his shoulder to make sure the football player wasn't following him. "Can we go home now?"

Chris nodded. "Yeah, I'm just waiting for — "

"Oh, no, here he comes!" Daryl said. "We have to get out of here!"

Chris turned and saw the football player barreling toward them. Was this night *ever* going to end? "Sarah! Brad! Come on!"

Dan intercepted her on the way to the door. "Here." He shoved some money into her hand. "Sorry, I could only get twenty-five more."

"No, that's great," Chris said, delighted. "Thank you." She looked back, seeing that the football player was almost upon them. "Sorry, we have to go!"

"Wait," Dan said, trying to stop them. "I'll drive you."

"You'll *what*?" Brad said.

"I'll drive you." Dan ushered them all outside, slamming the door in the surprised football player's face. "Come on, let's go."

Chapter 16

Dan had a Jeep — a very *nice* Jeep. They all piled in; Brad sulkily, everyone else with enthusiasm.

"So." Dan started the engine. "Where we headed?"

"Um, Lower Wacker Drive," Chris said. "Is that near here?"

Dan nodded, signaled, then pulled out.

"This is great," Daryl said to Brad. "A ride from someone normal and *everything*!"

"Yeah." Brad scowled. "Mr. Hero to the rescue."

Lower Wacker Drive was an underground street, almost a tunnel. On one side, it was bordered by the Chicago River; on the other side, there were exhaust-stained cement walls. The street was lit by greenish streetlights, giving it an eerie glow.

"This is weird," Dan said, driving slowly.

"Then you should feel right at home," Brad grumbled from the back.

They drove down a dark hill, Chris, Daryl, and Sarah craning out the windows for any sign of Dawson's Garage.

"Look," Chris said, finally seeing a red and amber neon sign that said "Dawson's Garage," with Pruitt's tow truck parked out in front. "That's it."

Dan pulled up in front of it, then helped Chris out of the car, the other three following.

"Hey, come on," Daryl said to Brad, putting his hand on his arm. "He seems like an okay guy."

"Mmmm," Brad said, not smiling.

To all appearances, the garage was deserted. The floor was covered with motor oil stains, with fan belts and other car parts lying all over the place. There were shelves along one wall, stacked with jugs of antifreeze and transmission fluid, as well as cans of oil.

"Hey, all *right!*" Daryl said, seeing the station wagon.

It was parked to one side, the windshield repaired, a brand new tire replacing the ruptured one.

"It *is* fixed," Chris said, very happy to see it. Feeling homesick, even.

"Where's Dawson?" Daryl asked.

"Who knows," Chris said. "Everybody into the car." She watched to make sure that they got in, then turned to Dan, suddenly feeling shy. "Well."

He smiled. "Well."

"I, uh — thanks," she said. "Really."

He shrugged. "I was glad to do it."

"Well, I don't know what we would have done."

"Oh, you probably would have figured something out," he said.

Chris smiled. "Something *complicated*, probably." She glanced at the station wagon, checking again to make sure it was really there, and that all three kids were inside. "Well," she said, "I guess I'd better — "

"I don't even know your name," Dan said.

"Oh. Right. Um, Chris Parker."

They smiled at each other.

"Go pay for the car," Dan said. "I'll wait here and make sure you get out okay."

"No, really," Chris said, shaking her head. "You can go. Everything's fine now. Really."

"You're sure?"

Chris nodded. "I'm sure."

"Okay, Chris Parker." He winked at her. "Drive safely."

She nodded. "I will."

He also nodded, bent toward her, hesitated, and moved back. "See you."

Chris watched him as he hopped into his

Jeep, waved at her, and drove away.

"Hey, wait!" She called after the Jeep. "How do I find you to pay you back?"

But he was already gone.

She walked over to the car, already missing this guy who had come into, and gone out of, her life so quickly. Seeing her expression, Brad smiled a little.

"Atta boy," Daryl said.

"Right," Brad said, looking embarrassed.

"Okay," Chris said, back to business. "We'll just find Dawson, and we're out of here."

There was a great clanging and banging above them, and they all jumped. Up in the ceiling, there seemed to be a lot of machinery, smoke, and steam billowing down.

"Hello?" Chris said, a little tentative.

The clanging was louder.

"Chris, this might be trouble," Brad said. "Maybe we should just go."

Chris weighed that, then shook her head. "Hello?"

A voice boomed out over the clanging. "What?!"

Chris glanced around. "Mr. Dawson?"

Out of the ceiling, a giant hydraulic lift descended, the smoke and steam increasing, Chris backing out of the way. As the lift came down, they could see a man standing on it. He was tall and muscular, with long, blond hair. He was wearing a black T-shirt, jeans, and heavy boots. And, in one hand, he held a thick, battered, black sledgehammer.

Sarah gasped, leaping out of the car. "It's *Thor*," she said, awestruck.

Chapter 17

Before Chris could stop her, Sarah ran up to the man, hugging his leg.

"Thor!" she said happily. "I *knew* we'd find you!"

The man looked down at her uneasily. "Who is this kid?"

Chris pulled Sarah away. "You're Mr. Dawson, right?"

The man nodded.

"Secret identity," Sarah whispered to Daryl.

Dawson climbed off the lift. "What do you kids want?"

"Well, Mr. Pruitt sent us." Chris indicated the station wagon. "That's our car over there."

"Oh," Dawson said. "You owe me fifty bucks."

Chris handed him the money, which he counted.

Sarah moved closer, watching him with adoring eyes. "Have you been fighting the Forces of Darkness?"

Dawson stopped counting. "What's she talking about?"

"She thinks you're somebody else," Brad said.

"It's him, Brad!" Sarah insisted. "It's really him!" She leaned closer to Dawson. "Don't listen to my brother — he said you were a jerk, anyway."

Dawson looked at Brad, his eyes narrowing. "You said *what*, kid?"

"Nothing," Brad said quickly. "I just — I told you. She's — confused."

"Unh-hunh." Dawson looked at him suspiciously, then went back to counting the money. "Hey, what is this?" He held it up. "This is only forty-five. You owe me *fifty*."

Chris shrugged helplessly. "I'm sorry. We don't have it."

"Then you don't have the car." He slapped the money into her hand and turned to go.

Sarah stared at him, horrified. "But — but you're — "

"How could you do this to us?" Chris asked, drowning her out. "For five lousy dollars?"

Dawson climbed onto the lift. "I'd do it for five lousy *cents*." His face hardened. "Now, get out of here."

"You don't understand," Chris said. "We've had the worst — "

Dawson cut her off. "This is a garage, kid, not a confessional. Five dollars, or get out."

They were all stunned, no one more so than Sarah.

"Is — is Thor kicking us out?" she asked.

Chris nodded. "Yes, Sarah."

Sarah ran over to him, tugging at his shirt. He looked down, brushing her off impatiently, as Sarah looked up at him with her eyes filled with tears.

"I-I thought you *always* helped people in trouble," she said.

He pushed her away. "This is the city, kid. I don't help anybody but myself."

"But — "

"Get *lost*," he said.

Bursting into tears, Sarah ran to Chris, then remembered something and, taking off her winged helmet, ran back to Dawson. "Wait!"

He turned off the lift control, scowling at her.

"I know why you're not acting like yourself," she said. "You don't have your special helmet."

"My *what*?"

She held the winged helmet up to him, having to stand on her tiptoes. "Here, take mine."

Dawson hesitated.

"Go on," she said. "Take it."

"Y-you're giving me this?" he asked. "For nothing?"

"Well, yeah." Sarah beamed at him. "You're my hero!"

Overcome with warmth, Dawson reached down and took the helmet. He looked at it, touched, then reached into his pocket. He pulled out the car keys and flipped them to Chris.

"Go on," he said. "Take the car."

"Thank you," Chris said, hurrying over to it before he could change his mind.

Sarah leaned up, giving him a big hug and kiss. "Thanks, Thor. I knew you wouldn't let me down." She ran to the car, a huge smile on her face.

Dawson got off the lift, walking to the front of the garage to open the door for them. When it was all the way up, he paused by the car, while Chris rolled down her window. He looked at the helmet, looked at Sarah, then handed it in through the window. "Here," he said.

Sarah's smile got even bigger. "Thank you, Thor."

Chris handed him the forty-five dollars. "Take this."

He put it in his pocket and stepped aside as Chris drove out toward Lower Wacker Drive.

"What time is it?" she asked, checking both ways for traffic.

Daryl checked his watch. "Eleven-forty-five."

"All right," Chris said excitedly. "We can get Brenda and still be home by one. We can *do* this."

Sarah put on her helmet, lovingly adjusting the strap. "*Man*, I'm up late."

Chris turned to look at her. "Now I mean it. Lie down and get some sleep."

Sarah grinned and closed her eyes.

"Good." Chris put on the gas, and they sped down Lower Wacker Drive.

Behind them, in the shadows, Dan Lynch sat in his Jeep. He watched to make sure that they were on their way, nodded, and put the Jeep in gear, driving in the other direction.

Beyond him, also in the shadows, the black Lincoln Continental was parked. Joe Gipp sat sadly behind the wheel, Bleak and Graydon in the backseat.

"Okay, good work, Gipp," Bleak said. "Follow them."

Slowly, Joe Gipp started the car.

Chapter 18

It was eleven-forty-six, and at the bus station Brenda came out of the ladies' room, disgusted by the condition it was in. Lonely and aggravated, she made her way through a row of chairs to find an empty seat.

She heard snoring and stopped. Familiar snoring. She peered to look at the person in the chair below her, recognizing the blurry form of the bag lady who had stolen her glasses. And she was still wearing them.

Brenda leaned closer, checking to make sure she had the right person, then snatched the glasses off the woman's face.

The bag lady woke up instantly. "Thief! Stop, thief!"

Brenda turned to run, crashing right into one of the janitors who had caught the rat.

He grabbed her. "You stealing this lady's glasses?"

"No!" She tried to wrench free. "These are *my* glasses!"

An old man came lurching out of a nearby phone booth, pointing a quavering finger at Brenda. "She stole 'em! I saw her!"

"No, she stole them from *me*," Brenda said. "They're *my* glasses!"

"Tramp!" the bag lady screeched. "Thief! No good — "

The creepy man with the gun who Brenda had first seen when she was on the phone with Chris appeared. "What's going on?"

"Look out!" Brenda said. "He has a gun, I saw it!"

The creepy man pulled out his gun and whirled around, paranoid. "Who does? Where?"

The bag lady lunged for Brenda. "Gimme my glasses!"

Brenda twisted away from all of them, running for the bus station exit.

"Stop her!" the bag lady shrieked, and everyone within earshot started chasing her, most of them yelling, "Stop! Thief!"

Brenda ran out of the station and across the street, dodging traffic all the way, and ducking into a small dark alley. She hid behind a Dumpster, breathing hard, listening to see if they had followed her. When she didn't hear anything, she relaxed a little and put the fingerprint-smeared glasses on, seeing clearly — sort of — for the first time in hours.

Hours. Where *was* Chris, anyway?

"Oh, *look*," Sarah said, as they drove past a huge toy store. "*Look* at all that!" She pressed her nose against the car window, admiring the colorful display of toys. "Wow."

The stoplight ahead was yellow, and Chris started to speed up, saw that she wouldn't make it, and stopped for the red light.

"Great," she said, tapping her fingers on the steering wheel. "Like we have time to waste."

"We'll make it," Daryl said, checking his watch.

"We'd better," Chris said. "If we don't, we're all — " She stopped, staring at the building on their left.

Brad and Daryl looked over, too, Sarah still captivated by the toy store on the other side of the street.

The building was Le Ciel Bleu, the restaurant every bit as elegant as Chris had known it would be, the parking lot crowded with shiny, expensive cars.

"What are we looking at?" Brad asked.

Chris sighed, thinking of Mike, she realized, for the first time in several hours.

"Mike and I were supposed to go there tonight."

"Kind of looks like he went without you," Daryl said.

Chris sat bolt upright. "What?"

Daryl pointed. "Check it out."

There was a red Firebird parked in the lot.

"Oh, come on, that could be — " Chris stopped, seeing that the license plate was "SO COOL."

"What's wrong?" Brad asked, seeing her face go pale.

"Everything," Chris said, and stamped on the gas pedal, swerving the car into the parking lot. "Stay here," she said and jumped out of the car.

Brad looked at Daryl. "You going to stay here?"

"No way," Daryl said, already opening his door. "Come on!"

Chris stalked up to the front door, throwing it open. It was, indeed, a very elegant restaurant, the lights romantically low, the well-dressed customers being served by waiters in black tie.

The maitre d' glanced up from his reservation book, frowning when he saw Chris and the kids, all of whom looked worn and disheveled.

"May I help you?" he asked, his voice icy.

Chris searched behind him for a sign of

Mike, her lips pressed tightly together. "Just looking for someone, thanks."

The maitre d' frowned, but went back to his reservation book.

Chris scanned the tables, seeing a lot of wealthy faces, eating various sauce-covered meals, *not* seeing Mike — then, she found him, sitting on the side, looking quite dashing in his sport coat and tie. He was sitting at a small table, with a dazzling bleached-blonde girl in a skin-tight white dress. Apparently, their dinners had just arrived, and they were lifting their champagne glasses in a toast.

Chris leaned back against the wall, not quite ready to believe her eyes. "He's with Sesame Plexar, he — " She shook her head. Snapping out of it, she said, "What a *scuzz*."

Sarah snared a chocolate pastry from a nearby cart. "Sesame?" she asked with her mouth full. "Like *Sesame Street*?"

"Like 'I.Q. of a sesame seed,'" Brad said.

"Wow." Daryl shook his head. "He dumps you for *that*, and you get a night of terror. Doesn't seem fair to me."

"Me?" Brad said. "I'd kill him."

Chris looked tempted, but shook her head. "I don't have time."

Daryl set his watch from eleven-fifty-seven back to eleven-forty-two, then shoved it under Chris's nose. "You've got time," he said. "Besides, this whole *night* was his fault."

Chris nodded, furious now. "You bet it

was." She spun around to face Brad. "You stay here. Watch Sarah. I'll be right back." She squared her shoulders, took a deep breath, and strode into the dining area.

"This," Brad said quietly, "I have to see."

Chapter 19

Outside, the Lincoln Continental was parked at the curb across the street.

"What're they doing in there?" Graydon asked.

Bleak smiled a small, cruel smile. "Just be patient."

Still behind the wheel, Joe Gipp pulled out a bandana, mopping it across his forehead.

Inside, Mike and Sesame were cuddling up together, paying much more attention to each other than they were to their very expensive dinners.

"You know," Mike said, touching her hair, "girls like you come along once in a lifetime."

"Or twice in the same night," Chris said, standing behind him with her arms folded.

Mike froze, his hand still on Sesame's hair.

"How's your sister?" Chris asked, her voice dangerously sweet. "All better?"

"Uh — I — " he started.

"You lied," Chris said.

"No, I — " He coughed. "I didn't — "

"*Don't* lie!" Chris said.

Everyone in the restaurant stopped talking, and looked over at their table.

Mike stood up, lowering his voice. "Come on, Chris, okay? Get a grip."

"A grip?" she said, almost shouting. "Do you have *any* idea of what I've been through tonight!"

The restaurant was very quiet, customers still holding their forks in midair, waiters holding heavy trays.

"I thought — " Chris swallowed, closer to tears than she had expected. "I thought you loved me. Was all that — what you said, all that was — you were lying, right?"

Mike grabbed her arm. "Listen, little girl," he said furiously. "I don't know what you thought we had, but it wasn't even *half* as serious as you'd like to think it was!"

Suddenly, Brad and Daryl were there, Brad's fists clenched.

"Let her go," he said.

Mike sneered, dropping her arm. "Picking them kinda young, aren't you, Chris?"

"This kid's got more class at fourteen than you'll *ever* have," Chris said.

Mike smirked. "Be my guest, kid. She's not worth it, anyway."

Brad kicked him as hard as he could, resulting in Mike's doubling over in agony, and Sesame's screaming in either terror or sympathy.

"*You're* not worth it, buddy," Brad said.

"*And* you have an ugly car. This is for last summer." Daryl kicked him, too, knocking him over.

"See you around, Mike," Chris said, looking down at him on the floor, trying to get up. "Life's too short to waste on losers like you."

She turned and headed for the door, Brad and Daryl behind her, customers and waiters alike applauding. Even the maitre d' clapped.

Once they were outside, Chris and the boys exchanged high fives.

"Yo, we were *ex*cellent!" Daryl said.

Brad grinned. "We were, weren't we?"

"We certainly were," Chris said. "In *fact* — " She stopped, realizing something, looking around in panic. "Where's Sarah? Has anyone seen Sarah?"

Down the block, Sarah stood transfixed in front of the toy-store window, her hands and face smeared with chocolate as she finished up the last of her French pastry. She skated back and forth along the display windows, looking at everything, singing "The Baby-sitting Blues" to herself.

Then, she saw two new reflections in the

window, recognizing Bleak and Graydon.
Slowly, she turned to face them.

"You like toys, little girl?" Bleak asked,
with a Grinch-like smile.

Graydon lunged forward to grab her knapsack, and Sarah ducked under his arms, skating away like lightning.

"Come on!" Bleak said, running back to
the Lincoln. He jumped in, slapping Joe Gipp
on the shoulder, pointing at the distant skating figure. "*Get* her," he said.

Joe Gipp stepped on the gas.

Hearing the car behind her, Sarah skated
as fast as she could, cutting down an alley,
her eyes watering from the wind. She saw
a familiar building up ahead and relaxed. It
was the Associates' Building.

"Mom! Dad!" she said and skated even
more quickly.

Brad ran up to the toy store, Chris and
Daryl just behind him.

"Oh, no," he said, out of breath. "I thought
she'd be here, I thought — "

They all turned, hearing brakes squeal,
and saw the Lincoln Continental careening
down an alley.

"Oh, *no*," Chris said, and they started running again.

Sarah skated toward the revolving doors

of the Associates' Building, the Lincoln veering up over the sidewalk after her. Graydon jumped out, grabbing her cape just as she skated into the doorway. Her momentum spun the door so that his arm got stuck. She was stuck; Graydon was stuck; and Bleak shoved on the door, trying to knock them free, Graydon screaming in protest.

The front lobby was empty, except for a workman pushing an electric floor polisher across the new tile. He stared at what was happening, dumbfounded, then ran over to help.

Sarah pushed the door as hard as she could, just as Graydon yanked the cape right off her shoulders, falling backward onto the sidewalk. Bleak shouldered past him and into the revolving doors, but Sarah was already free, skating inside and past the startled workman.

"Hey, kid!" he said. "You can't — "

Sarah skated into the only open elevator just as Bleak and Graydon blasted through the revolving doors and into the lobby. Frantically, Sarah punched at two of the floor buttons, neither of them responding.

The workman stepped out to block Bleak and Graydon. "What's going on here?"

Bleak drew his fist back, knocking the man down with one hard right before continuing on his way. The elevator doors closed just as he and Graydon got to them, and as it rose up, Sarah could hear the two men shouting threats. Ugly threats.

The elevator rose up and up, Sarah pushing the two buttons to try to stop it, without success. Finally, the elevator stopped, opening into a dark unfinished penthouse, the walls plastered, but not covered, the cement floor uncarpeted. Sarah skated out, expecting to see her parents' party.

"Daddy!" she yelled, just in case. "Help!"

There was no answer. She was definitely on the wrong floor. She turned back to the elevator, but the doors had already closed, the elevator going back down.

Sarah looked around, deciding not to panic yet. There was a door marked Stairs, and she skated over to it, finding it locked. And there weren't any other doors.

Now she could panic. She was trapped.

Chapter 20

Downstairs, Bleak and Graydon waited impatiently for the elevator. It finally came and they jumped on.

"Now what?" Graydon asked.

Bleak studied the buttons, seeing that two of them were smeared with chocolate. He pushed both of them. "I'll take this floor, you take the one above."

The elevator stopped at a well-lit floor, the sounds of a party with a cocktail pianist wafting out. Cautiously, Bleak stepped out of the elevator.

He passed the coat-check room — which was empty — and walked down a narrow corridor to the party itself, seeing a crowd of elegantly dressed men and women. He scowled at the sight, darting his eyes back and forth, looking for Sarah. There were no children, only adults — gathered around the piano player, singing along, and mingling in small groups.

A jovial tuxedoed man wandered over. "Hey, there." He slung his arm over Bleak's shoulders. "I hate to see people alone at a party. Gets me depressed. C'mon, I'll introduce you to some of my friends." Before Bleak could protest, the man pulled him over to one of the groups.

The elevator doors opened at the penthouse and Graydon crept out, moving into the shadows to look for Sarah, taking it one room at a time.

In the farthest room, one whole wall was made up of glass, the city glittering far below. Construction equipment was piled up against the other three walls: bags of plastic, spools of wires, coils of cable and rope — and Sarah.

She crouched down behind three dusty bags of cement, trying not to sneeze as a cold draft wafted a cloud of dust off one bag. Not sure why there would be a draft, she looked around, seeing that there was a large rectangle of open space in the glass wall where a window was missing. A sheet of opaque plastic was taped over it, but the wind was riffling against it, the plastic flapping slightly. From somewhere faraway, Sarah could hear faint city street sounds.

Then, she heard another sound. Like a footstep. She looked at the door to the next room, seeing a slow-moving shadow passing the wedge of light under the door.

She swallowed, terrified, pushing back against the wall to make herself smaller, her back curled into a large, elbow-jointed pipe that ran into the wall.

The footsteps in the other room were louder, closer, and she looked at the open window. Then at the door. Then at one of the coils of rope. She had a plan.

Not finding her in the room he was in, Graydon opened the door to the last room, a breeze hitting him in the face. He walked all the way in, methodically searching among the pieces of equipment, bending down to look behind the bags of cement.

There, he saw a rope knotted childishly, but securely, around the elbow-jointed pipe. The rope ran up behind the construction equipment, stretched taut, then disappeared out the open window.

"No," he said. "She *couldn't* have." He ran to the open glass and looked down.

He saw Sarah, a floor below, inching down the rope, seventy stories above the street.

Hearing a noise, Sarah looked up, so scared that she almost let go of the rope when she saw who was staring down at her.

* * *

Brad stood in front of the Associates' Building, looking at the sidewalk. Behind him, Chris and Daryl were still searching in doorways, behind parked cars, in trashcans, calling Sarah's name every few seconds.

"You guys, come quick!" Brad yelled, finding his voice.

They ran over, stopping when they saw Sarah's cape, lying on the sidewalk in front of the revolving doors. Inside the lobby, a workman lay unconscious, his floor polisher moving around the floor unguided.

An empty Lincoln Continental was parked at the curb.

Brad swallowed. "Sarah's in trouble."

"Sarah's in *big* trouble," Chris said, and they all ran into the building.

Up in the penthouse, Graydon pulled on the rope, dragging Sarah up the glass. Sarah kept climbing down, two feet for every foot he hauled her up, her sneakers squeaking against the glass. He kept pulling; she kept climbing down, gradually running out of rope.

When it was almost gone, she took a deep breath — and let go. The weight gone, Graydon fell back onto the floor. He scrambled up, looking out the window to see Sarah pressed against the glass of the floor below, her fingers digging into the thin window ledge.

She hung on as tightly as she could, looking down only once. It was a long, long drop.

Above her, very shaky, Graydon climbed out of the window, clinging to the rope, descending in her direction.

Seeing Graydon climbing toward her, Sarah inched along the window ledge, away from him, completely terrified. He was much closer now, and she closed her eyes, very aware of the street below.

"Forces of Darkness beware," she whispered. "The Forces of Light are here." Saying the words gave her courage, and she continued along the window ledge.

In the elevator, Chris pressed one of the chocolate-smeared buttons and when the doors opened, all three of them ran out, stopping when they heard the piano playing, and the voices talking and laughing.

"I don't believe it," Chris said. "We're *at* your parents' party."

Daryl covered his eyes with his arm, as though that would keep him from being recognized. "We've had it. We've really had it."

There was a coatroom to their left, and Chris dragged the boys into it, hiding them behind cashmere and camel hair coats, as far back as they could go.

"Look," Brad said. "Maybe we should just give up."

"No way!" Daryl burrowed deeper into the coats. "Not me!"

"Not without Sarah," Chris said. "You guys stay here, and I'll get her back."

"*Then* let's give up," Brad said.

"No, *then* let's get out of here," Daryl said. "We've come too far to get ourselves killed by our own parents."

Brad saw the logic in that and nodded. "You're right. Get her, Chris."

"Stay here," she warned them, and slunk down the corridor toward the party.

She took refuge behind a large potted plant, scanning the guests for Sarah. Not seeing her, she came out from behind the plant, staying low, hiding behind the buffet table.

In the hall, Mr. Anderson was just coming out of the men's room, whistling. He headed right for the coat room. Brad's and Daryl's eyes widened as they saw him, and they pressed further into the coats.

Mr. Anderson came all the way into the coatroom, apparently looking for his wife's coat and his own, sliding back hangers as he searched.

Brad and Daryl exchanged a look, Brad biting his lip in indecision. Daryl brought his finger to his own lips, pleading with Brad to stay quiet. Brad hesitated, then nodded, and they held their breaths, waiting to be discovered.

But Mr. Anderson found the two coats,

127

took them from the hangers, and left, still whistling.

"Whew," Daryl said, sinking down.

"It's not over *yet*," Brad said.

Out in the main room, Chris moved on her hands and knees behind the bar, seeing nothing but the bank of sloping windows, darkness beyond. She peered out around the bar to see the party from a different angle. Still no Sarah.

Something tapped her shoulder and she flinched, looking up.

"Looking for someone?" Bleak asked, standing above her. Smiling.

Chapter 21

At that moment, Mrs. Anderson stepped up to the bar with her husband, both of them holding their coats. The angle of the bar was high enough so that they couldn't see Chris crouched down behind it.

"You told Chris one o'clock," Mr. Anderson said.

Recognizing the voice, Chris cringed lower, her face just above Bleak's shoelaces. She smiled, getting an idea.

"Don't worry, we'll make it," Mrs. Anderson said. She smiled at Bleak. "Excuse me."

"What?" he asked.

"Champagne, please," she said.

He looked at her blankly.

Finished with tying Bleak's shoelaces together, Chris glanced up at the windows, seeing Sarah inching her way across the glass in full view of the party. If any of the guests happened to look over there — luckily, most of them were gathered around the piano, or deep in conversation.

Sarah was obviously almost crying, looking above her to something Chris couldn't see, and Chris realized that she must have gone outside from the floor above.

"Are you okay, pal?" Mr. Anderson asked Bleak, who had yet to move.

Seizing the moment, Chris crawled out from behind the bar, darting behind the buffet table before anyone could see her. She ran from it, to the plant, and then back toward the coatroom.

"Excuse me," Bleak said, the only one to see her go. "I'll have to get another bottle." He turned to leave, his tied-together shoelaces sending him crashing to the floor.

Chris rushed into the coatroom. "You guys, quick!"

Both boys sprang out, hearing the urgency in her voice.

"What?" Brad asked. "What is it?"

"She's out!" Chris said. "Out the window! *Outside*!"

They ran to the elevator, which was still open, Chris hitting the other chocolate-smeared button.

"How — " Brad started.

"She went upstairs," Chris said, frantic. "Upstairs and out!"

Sarah clung to the glass for dear life, looking inside at all of the party guests, none of whom saw her. Including her parents.

Graydon had left the rope now and was moving slowly toward her, his grip just as precarious, but he was getting closer to her every second.

The elevator doors opened and Chris and the boys ran into the penthouse, following the breeze to the room with the open window. They saw the rope leading out of it and dashed over, looking down to see Graydon reaching out to grab Sarah, the rope swinging free above him.

Chris leaned out and grabbed the rope, swinging it toward Sarah. "Sarah! Grab the rope!"

Sarah looked up and saw them, smiled, and quickly grabbed the rope, looping it around her waist.

"Okay," Chris said to the boys. *"Pull!"*

Using all of their weight, they pulled as hard as they could, dragging Sarah to safety.

"Oh, thank God," Chris said, hugging her.

"Can we go home now?" Sarah asked, her voice very small.

"Not yet," someone behind them said, and they turned to see Joe Gipp, with his hand out.

"W-what are you going to do?" Daryl

asked, moving away from the temptingly open window.

"Look, I'm not going to hurt you," Joe said. "I just want the magazine."

"What magazine?" Chris asked.

"The one you stole from the office."

"What," Daryl said, "you guys too cheap to buy another one?"

"Just give it to me," Joe said patiently, "okay?"

Daryl unzipped Sarah's knapsack, taking out the *Playboy* and handing it to him. Joe opened it to the centerfold, Chris covering Sarah's eyes.

"This is what they're after," he said, indicating the handwriting. "Just some notes. Stuff we need."

"You mean, that was *it*?" Brad said. "*That* was why you were chasing us?"

Joe nodded.

"*Anyway*," Chris changed the subject, motioning out the window, "what about him?"

Joe shrugged, tossing the rope back out. "Leave 'im hanging for a while, let him sweat it out. In the meantime, let's get you guys out of here."

As the elevator started down, Joe shook his head.

"You were right," he said. "Babysitting *is* dangerous."

Chris laughed. "*That's* for sure."

The doors opened on the next floor, Bleak

standing there, waiting to get in, stunned to see them already in there.

"Hold the elevator please?" Mr. Anderson called from down the hall.

"Oh, *no*," Brad said. "That's my parents."

Daryl sat down on the floor, covering his head. "I *knew* we weren't going to make it."

"Yeah, you are," Joe said and punched Bleak in the jaw just as he was starting to react, the doors closing before the Andersons got to them.

Mr. and Mrs. Anderson looked at Bleak lying on the floor, then looked at each other in confusion, hearing a wild cheer erupt from the rapidly descending elevator.

Chapter 22

After making sure that everyone was in the station wagon and wearing seat belts, Chris sped to the bus station, skidding to a stop just in front of it.

"With *our* luck, she's probably gone by now," Daryl said.

Across the street, still hiding, Brenda saw the car and ran over, banging on Chris's window. Then she ran around to the passenger's side, jumping in.

"Oh, boy," she said, out of breath and nearly sobbing. "You won't *believe* what happened to me tonight!"

They all looked at her, not impressed.

"*Everything* happened," she said and started crying.

More as a nervous release than anything else, Chris started laughing. Sarah joined in, and within a few seconds, all of them were laughing, so hard that the car was shaking, so hard that they couldn't stop.

When everyone had calmed down — which took a while — Chris headed straight for the expressway and the suburbs. She drove quickly, but carefully, Brad sitting next to her. The others were in the backseat, Brenda sleeping against the window.

"My hammer!" Sarah yelled suddenly. She scrambled around the backseat, searching for it. "It's not here!"

Chris sighed. "You must have left it someplace."

"We have to go back and find it," Sarah said, nearly hysterical.

"Sarah, honey, we can't," Chris said. "I mean — where would we *start*?"

"I lost my hammer," Sarah said, about to cry.

"At least you got your cape," Daryl pointed out, since it had still been lying on the sidewalk when they left the building.

"Besides," Brad said. "You met Thor."

"Yeah." She cheered up instantly. "I did."

Chris smiled, relieved that the crisis was over. "Daryl, what time is it?"

He frowned at his incorrect watch. "I don't know. A little after one, I think."

Chris stepped on the gas. "We still have a chance."

Mr. and Mrs. Anderson drove down the

expressway, going as fast as the law would allow. A station wagon packed with kids sped past them, too dark inside for any of the faces to be visible.

Mrs. Anderson shook her head. "It scares me to think Brad and Sarah are going to be driving someday with people like that on the road."

Mr. Anderson nodded. "Me, too."

When Chris finally pulled into the driveway, everyone leaped out of the car, running for the front door. Chris stopped, clapping her hands for attention.

"Brad! Daryl! Sarah! Upstairs! *Now*!" She ordered. "Brenda! Go home!"

"But — " Brenda started.

Chris shoved her out of the house. "Go home, I'll talk to you tomorrow, okay?"

"Yeah, but — " Brenda frowned. "What *happened* to you guys tonight?"

"Later!" Chris said, and slammed the door. She shoved the kids toward the stairs. "Quick, everybody into pajamas!"

"I don't have any here," Daryl said.

"I don't care! Upstairs, *go*!"

The kids ran upstairs, and Chris tore into the kitchen, where the macaroni was still all over the counter. She grabbed every free dish in sight, throwing them into the sink, running hot water over them. Then, she snatched up a sponge, cleaning wildly. She heard a car pull into the driveway and worked faster.

She was almost finished, hearing the car drive into the garage, when she dropped a bottle of Fantastik, half of it spilling out across the floor. She dropped to her knees, scrubbing at the liquid with paper towels.

She bundled everything disposable into the trash can, and then, hearing the car doors slam, gave the spotless kitchen one quick look, then threw the sponge into the sink and ran into the living room.

She turned on the television and dove onto the couch, just as Mr. and Mrs. Anderson walked into the kitchen. She grabbed a magazine from the coffee table, opened it to the middle, and slouched over it as Mr. and Mrs. Anderson stepped into the living room.

"Hi," Mrs. Anderson said. "Sorry we're late."

Chris put the magazine down with a glazed smile. "No problem," she said.

"Any excitement tonight?" Mr. Anderson asked.

"Not really," Chris said, evenly. "Brad stayed home. Daryl slept over here."

"Oh, honey," Mrs. Anderson said. "What a nightmare for you."

Chris managed a very weak grin.

Chapter 23

On the excuse of "needing to get something," Chris went upstairs, letting herself into Brad's room. He and Daryl were bundled up on the floor in blankets, watching *Creeping Terror* on a small television, which they turned down when they saw her.

"What happened?" Brad whispered.

"Everything's cool," Chris whispered back.

Sarah, wearing her nightgown, slipped into the room. "Can we do this again next Friday?" she asked, also whispering.

Chris had to laugh. "Forget it, Sarah. I'm retired."

"No, please," Sarah said. "You *have* to sit for me again."

"We'll see," Chris said gently.

No one said anything for a minute.

"Chris?" Brad asked.

She looked over. "Yeah?"

"I know seniors don't hang out with fourteen-year-olds, so if I say 'hi' or something in school and," he shifted slightly, "you ignore me like usual — well, that's okay, okay?"

Chris smiled at him. "I don't ignore friends, Brad."

He smiled back.

"*Well*," Daryl said, interrupting a potentially tender moment, "I just want to say thanks for giving me what was probably the greatest night of my life. So far."

"Me, too," Sarah said.

Brad nodded. "Me, too."

"Yeah." Chris had to agree with them. "Me, too."

Later, after saying good-bye to Mr. and Mrs. Anderson, Chris stepped outside, taking a deep breath of the night air. She reached inside her purse for her keys, coming out with her college applications. She looked at them, smiled, and tucked them back in.

Headlights swept across the driveway and Chris shielded her eyes with her hand, seeing a Jeep pull up in front of the house. And Dan Lynch getting out of it.

"Hi," he said.

"Hi." She stared at him, struck dumb by surprise. "How — I mean, how did you — "

He held up Sarah's plastic sledgehammer, the address label prominent. "I think the little girl might be missing this. She left it in the backseat."

Chris took it from him, dazed. "I-I can't

believe you came all the way out here to return this."

"Actually . . ." he said.

Her face fell. "You came for the money."

"No," he said. "I'm looking for a babysitter."

She shook her head. "Sorry. I think tonight was my last gig."

"Really?" he said. "That's too bad."

"Who was the babysitter for?" she asked.

He shrugged. "Me."

"Oh." She felt a smile coming. "Maybe retirement can wait."

Their eyes met and they exchanged smiles, Dan moving a little closer. They stood there, both hesitant.

"*Kiss him!*" Brad, Sarah and Daryl said, hanging out of an upstairs window, very amused by this whole scene.

Chris and Dan both laughed.

"What do you think?" he asked.

"It sounds good to me," she said.

They turned to each other and kissed.

Upstairs, Brad moved Sarah and Daryl away from the window, then closed it, slowly pulling the shade down.

One by one, the lights in the house went out, leaving the yard in darkness. Dan and Chris stood by his Jeep, holding each other.

What had started out as the worst night of her life really *had* changed into the best night of her life.